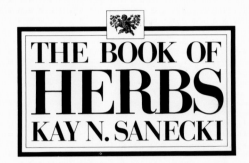

THE BOOK OF
HERBS
KAY N. SANECKI

THE BOOK OF
HERBS
KAY N. SANECKI

CHARTWELL
BOOKS, INC.

Written with love for

Robin and Timothy

who wish to learn about plants

A QUINTET BOOK

Published by Chartwell Books Inc.,
A Division of Book Sales Inc.,
110 Enterprise Avenue,
Secaucus, New Jersey 07094

ISBN 0-89009-855-7

Reprinted 1987

This book was designed and produced by
Quintet Publishing Limited
6 Blundell Street, London N7

Art design by Bridgewater Associates
Editor Stephen Paul

Typeset in Great Britain by
Q.V. Typesetting Limited, London
Color origination in Hong Kong by
Universal Colour Scanning Limited
Printed in Hong Kong by Leefung-Asco
Printers Limited

Acknowledgements

All pictures are reproduced by courtesy of
the Iris Hardwick Library of Photographs except for
the following: **13** The Royal Horticultural Society,
The Lindley Library, **26, 28-31,**
33 (below right) R.W. Peplow, **27** Practical Gardening

The illustrations are by Lorraine Harrison

CONTENTS

Introduction

ERB growing currently enjoys immense popularity. The renewed interest so apparent in the second half of the twentieth century began in America in the 1950s and spread quickly. The two-way exchange of plants between the Old and the New World began with the sixteenth century voyages that preceded the founding of Jamestown. During the first hundred years of settlement (mainly in New England and Virginia), many plants that Europeans had cultivated and used for centuries were imported — herbs, fruit trees, vegetables and many flowering bulbs.

The colonists took their books by Gerard, Parkinson and Culpeper with them from England and sent for seeds and roots to maintain their households, while they explored the wealth of economic plants of the New World. Much of what we know of herbs grown in America at that time is gleaned from contemporary accounts and such notes and papers as have been preserved. Perhaps the most remarkable of these are the records of the Winthrop family (who were settlers from England) and the descriptions of John Josselyn, an English naturalist who voyaged backwards and forwards during the seventeenth century.

In England every homestead had its own supply of herbs, even if they were obtained from the fields, for flavourings and food and household remedies. These humble plants have served us throughout the centuries, and today the renewed interest in them centres particularly on their healing properties. As garden plants they have remained faithful, unassuming favourites.

During the seventeenth century in England, and in fact Europe generally, the excitement generated by plants from the far corners of the world began to turn scholars' minds to the study of botany and to the development of horticultural science. At the same time medicine was developing along an independent course, until the nineteenth century brought the manufacture of synthetic drugs. All the while herbs were cultivated in the kitchen gardens, along with the vegetables and other economic plants. Only in the present century, with the gradual awakening of interest in herbs as plants for their own delight, and even more recently as medicine and natural flavourings, have decorative herb gardens become such a popular style of gardening.

Gathered within these plots are the oldest of our friends, harbouring delights of fragrance known to our forbears and legends repeated to countless generations.

OPPOSITE *Red dead nettle* (Lamium purpureum) *drawn by Timothy Sheldrake for his* Botanicum Medicinale *(1759). He describes it as 'Under every Hedge & all Highway sides, at the beginning of Summer.' And its virtues as 'Used against Haemorrhagies; & outwardly Wounds & Inflammation.'*

5

5

6

7

5

3

2

*

4

*

dge.

1

Starting with Herbs

HE amateur gardener need not be afraid to embark upon herb growing, provided two factors can be fulfilled — a suitable soil and some shelter from prevailing winds. The first condition is the more easily achieved because most herbs can be cultivated in containers of some sort while the soil in the borders is being improved. But providing shelter without robbing the plot of too much light is not always as simple. Fences and hedges or some form of windbreak are required and in the long term, a hedge is probably best as it reduces the wind speed and provides framework necessary for the design while at the same time containing the aromatic qualities of the herbs on the air within the garden.

RIGHT *A narrow border at the base of a sunny wall affords the opportunity to start a limited collection of herbs. The beginner can be assured of success however limited the available space.*

PROPAGATION

At every stage of growth the plants ought to be labelled with their name, so it is a good idea to make a set of labels before embarking upon any propagation. Herbs with annual life cycles (A), such as dill, basil, caraway and borage, are raised each year from seed, or from self-sown seedlings that can be replanted in a preferred situation in the spring. Others usually take two summers to come into flower from seed, and are known as biennials (B); plants like angelica, foxglove and evening primrose. The majority are perennial (P) in habit; most of these can be raised from seed, although vegetative propagation from division of rootstock, offsets or cuttings is often less hazardous.

FAR LEFT *A small group of culinary herbs planted at random in the kitchen garden; allium, mint and summer savory.*
LEFT *Part of the miniature formal herb garden at the American Museum, Claverton Manor, Bath, which is contained in a small plot with a bee skep at the centre.*
BELOW *Block planting of herbs gives a patchwork effect, which may be extended or varied from one season to the next.*

SOWING SEED

Seed of almost all herbs is either available from specialist seedsmen, or it can be saved from the previous summer, or as a last resort begged from fellow herb lovers. To give the seedlings a good start sow the seeds in pots, seed pans or boxes in spring and thin out or prick off, harden them if necessary, and plant out of doors in early summer. In the warmer regions sowing *in situ* in early spring is the best way and there is not much to be gained by starting the seedlings off indoors early. Most herbs can be raised from seed sown once the soil has warmed up after the winter frosts, and a rule of thumb is to cover the seed with soil to a depth of two or three times their own diameter.

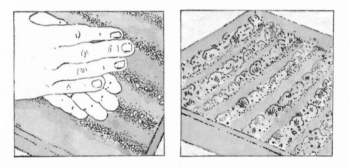

RIGHT *Once the seedlings have germinated and are large enough to handle, they can be thinned or transplanted to other boxes or pots. Delay at this stage results in plant losses, so move the baby plants on to encourage them to grow.*

LEFT *Use clean boxes or pots and fresh seed compost for raising seedlings. Sow the seed evenly and sparingly, either scattered all over the surface or, as here, in very shallow drills drawn across the surface of the compost.*

VEGETATIVE PROPAGATION

Herb plants that grow in clumps like chives, tarragon, bergamot, aconite and valerian need to be divided every three or four years or so into smaller clumps and replanted, in either the autumn (fall) or early spring. Cut back the top growth, sort out the roots, divide the clump into several pieces — each with a good root system — and replant firmly, at the same depth in the soil.

BELOW *A pair of garden forks, or even hand forks, can be used to divide large or stubborn perennial herb crowns. Plunge the forks back to back deep into the clump and then lever them apart. It is not always necessary to lift the old plant; portions can be removed independently in this way.*

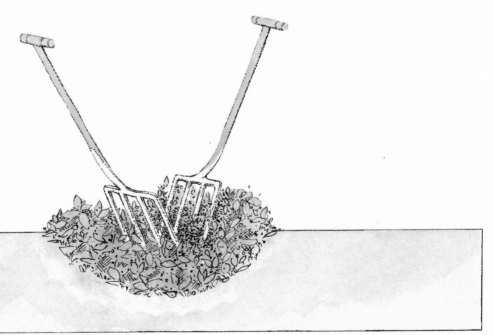

STEM CUTTINGS

Stem cuttings are usually taken from established perennial plants, and this method of propagation leaves the plants undisturbed. It is usual to take them in summer in England and in northern zones of America, or at any time in warmer areas provided that the plants are in active growth. Never take cuttings from plants, even evergreens, when they are dormant. The cuttings should develop small new roots within three to six weeks which stimulate leaf growth, and tiny new leaves soon become evident at the growing tips. Once the thrusting little root system has been formed the plants can be either potted up or put into a nursery bed (or kept under a plastic tunnel). In really chilly areas it is best to keep them in individual pots or plastic containers throughout their first winter.

RIGHT *Individual cuttings trimmed immediately below a node are inserted round the edge of the pot, into a proprietary cutting compost. A pencil-like stick or dibber is used to form the hole, and then to firm the compost round the cutting.*

RIGHT *A strong little root system should have developed. This tiny plant needs to be handled carefully so that the roots, and the soil adhering to them, are disturbed as little as possible.*

LEFT *From 3-6 weeks later, once there are signs of fresh growth at the tips, the cuttings need to be lifted gently, again, by the use of the dibber.*

LEFT *Plant each cutting individually, either into a small pot as here, or, if it needs protection through the winter, into a sheltered bed out of doors.*

ROOT CUTTINGS

Root cuttings or offsets can be taken from any herb plant that habitually runs about, sending up new shoots around the parent plant, such as elecampane, mint, horehound and yarrow. Most of the new shoots can be cut away in spring once growth starts. Where low temperatures are expected, and in cooler regions, break away any spreading roots at the end of the summer or in the autumn (fall). Cut them into pieces about 5 cms (2 ins) in length, place them flat on the soil surface in a box or seed pan and cover the whole with a plastic bag. The compost used needs to be light and topped with clean, fine horticultural sand. The boxes can then stay out of doors in all but the coldest regions, where they should be kept in a porch or cold greenhouse, or under a plastic tunnel until spring. Once little shoots appear, the bags should be removed and later the plants can be placed in their permanent positions. The overwintering of young plants is easy in temperate zones but where winter temperatures can be expected to fall below −5°C/20°F it is sometimes advisable not to try to propagate from root cuttings, but to follow some alternative method of propagation.

BUYING PLANTS

Perhaps it seems odd to say that when plants are bought already established in their pots or plastic containers, the first essential is to see that they are, in fact, properly identified. Many a herb gardener has planted out a young seedling believing it to be one thing, only to realize as it develops that it is something else. The next essential when choosing plants at the garden store or herb nursery is to examine them for general health, cleanliness and freedom from disease and insect attack. Select plants that are short jointed, not in flower and of a good colour, and avoid those whose roots are wandering out of the container at the base — these have been potted up rather a long time!

Making a Herb Garden

O special knowledge or skills are needed to grow herbs. They are accommodating and undemanding plants and as long as the general rules of garden hygiene are adhered to and a weed-free soil provided, success can be expected. The size of the garden, be it culinary border or decorative herb garden, depends on personal requirement and the space and funds available. The golden rule, however, is to keep it simple. European gardens in medieval times included the bulk of those plants which we today call herbs, and were then made up of a series of rectangular beds each containing one sort of plant. Today's version of this is the chess board idea of plant and pave, which is simplicity itself to make and manage.

ABOVE *A contemporary print of a 17th-century garden enclosed by railings with raised beds of various shapes containing herbs and other plants.*

PLANT AND PAVE

The basic area to be cultivated is divided into squares, and each alternate square — corresponding to the black squares of the chess board — is set with a single paving slab, or turfed, or even bricked. The spaces remaining — the white squares of the board — can then be planted with one herb each: marjoram, mint, dill, caraway; use several plants of each herb according to the size of the square. Where space is limited, or in a newly acquired garden in which the whole site is not ready, a few alternate squares treated in this way represent the beginning of a herb collection. It can be extended later with more paving and more plants. It is a particularly useful style of garden for informal areas, or for filling in awkward corners, offering a transition from lawn or driveway to border, and at the same time providing something easy to maintain and pleasing to the eye.

Where different levels have to be negotiated, the same overall alternate paving style can be used, ranging one or two rows above another. The alternating square effect may also be created by placing square containers each devoted to a single kind of plant in this chess board fashion.

LEFT, OPPOSITE *the simplicity of herbs is enhanced by some formal design. The cleanest is achieved by the use of square paving stones, brick patterns or lawn turf, used alternately with the plants. With an uncomplicated design on a small scale there is no need to make heavy work of marking out the design. Canes or trails of sand or gravel will serve as a guide line. Time and effort spent in laying paving, and getting it level, or in creating warm effects with brick patterns for the basic design, is well spent in the herb garden.*

Plants can be varied from season to season, although the paving is permanent.
The possible variations on the theme of the basic chess-board idea are numerous, the only requisites being that the areas should be level and the pattern repetitive in both size and composition. Select plants that complement each other, either in flower colour or leaf form and unless the area is extensive, avoid tall-growing herbs such as fennel and angelica.

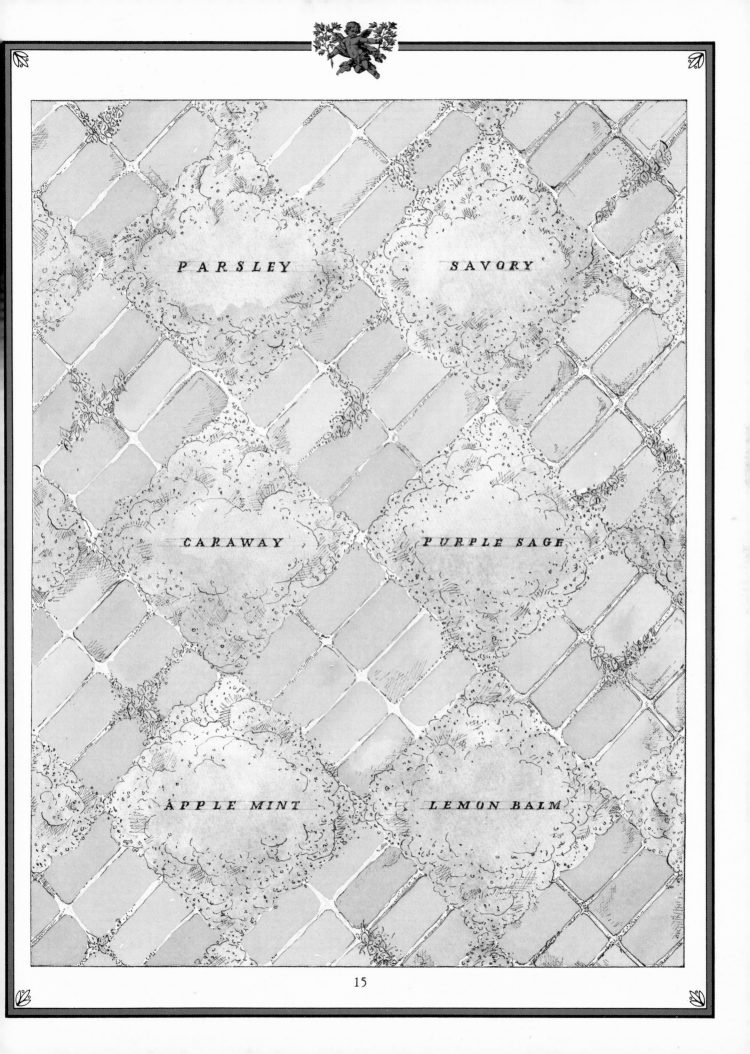

PARSLEY

SAVORY

CARAWAY

PURPLE SAGE

APPLE MINT

LEMON BALM

HERB BORDERS

Simplicity of planting is the key to success for the herb border. The border itself ought not to be too wide to allow ease of access and is best backed by a wall, fence or hedge to provide both shelter and good visual effect. Herbs themselves do not necessarily provide the most appropriate background hedge. A rose hedge is often too spreading, elder too hungry; rosemary, lavender and bay need protection themselves in all but the mildest areas and are not really winter hardy plants at all.

The less sophisticated the planting scheme the better, so that one plant will set off another or provide the complementary foil in leaf form, clump size or leaf colour for its neighbours. Low-growing plants like thyme, chives and marigolds need to be set towards the front of the border; the taller ones, like lovage, rosemary, fennel, angelica, at the back.

A formal effect in border planting can be introduced by making a formal edge with santolina, thyme or golden marjoram, or by placing paving stones in a diamond pattern near the front of the border. Both these ideas are rewarding when set along paths crossing a sloping site, or alongside a flight of steps.

RIGHT *Herbs can be gathered easily, as and when required from an informal border along a pathway in a kitchen garden.*

BELOW *Culinary herbs assembled in a sunny corner near the house will provide a constant supply of fresh flavourings all through the summer. The depth of the border must be in proportion with the scale of the garden and an edging of stones, a path or a lawn in front will add the trimness necessary to emphasize the abundance of the border. The tallest plants should be set at the back, with those of intermediate height and dumpy stature in front.*

Mint

Sage

House

Borage

Sweet Cicely

Border of Chives

Lemon Balm

Marjoram

Tarragon

Angelica

Thyme

Fennel

Lovage

Fence

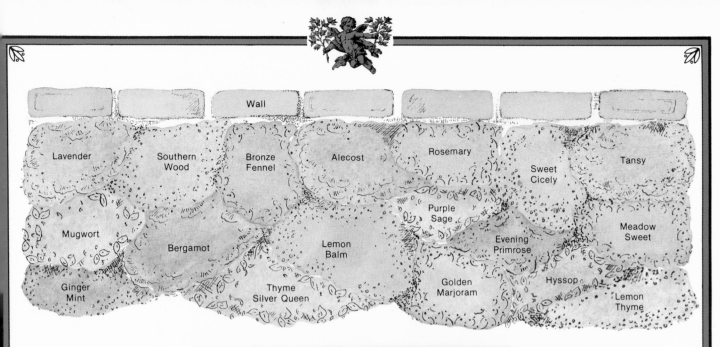

Wall

Lavender   Southern Wood   Bronze Fennel   Alecost   Rosemary   Sweet Cicely   Tansy

Mugwort   Bergamot   Lemon Balm   Purple Sage   Evening Primrose   Meadow Sweet

Ginger Mint   Thyme Silver Queen   Golden Marjoram   Hyssop   Lemon Thyme

ABOVE *A suggested plan for a border of aromatic herbs. Success will depend on good blocks of plants being massed, so that after the inevitable gaps of the first season, a fullness will develop. Put evenly matured plants of each kind in groups of three or five, except for the shrubs at the back, lavender, southernwood and rosemary, which are best planted individually and will soon fill their allotted space. Do not make the border too wide, otherwise maintenance will be a problem and the overall effect will lack decorative appeal.*

Quite unpromising sites can be transformed into herb gardens, which once established, need comparatively little attention during the growing season.
LEFT *Borage flourishes in a newly constructed raised bed against a wall in a farm yard. The blue flowers proclaim that this is the chosen site for kitchen herbs next year!*
BELOW LEFT *Bold planting of herbs across a steep slope on either side of a flight of steps, demonstrates their decorative value. Great yellow-green mop heads of tall angelica at the back reduce the gradient visually and force the emphasis on to the hummocks of santolina at foot level.*

FORMAL DESIGNS

It has to be accepted that herbs can never be first class plants for dramatic garden effect. Their appeal lies in their Old World associations, their aroma and the very simplicity of the plants themselves. They have largely escaped the contriving hybridists. The most attractive herb gardens are therefore made by using a careful selection of herbs in a repeated design or a bold theme of formal beds. One of the simplest patterns can be achieved by setting wedge-shaped beds around a central feature to form a circular plot. Bricks set along the lines of the imaginary spokes and rim of a wheel produce a very satisfactory bed in which to plant radiating rows of herbs. Variations are possible too: fewer beds, octagonal plots, a central sundial, a beehive or birdbath surrounded by paving or chamomile lawn all work well as the focal point in a formal circular garden. The next progression is to set a square plot within it. Whenever possible, measure the plot first and draw out a general plan to scale on paper before marking it out on the ground. Once on the ground it is always a good idea to indicate paths and beds by rope or a garden hosepipe and to leave the design for a few days. This way, it can be viewed from the windows of the house, a wheelbarrow can be wheeled about to ensure that the paths can be negotiated, the sunlight and shadows can be watched, and annoying mistakes can be avoided.

Beds should be large enough not to give a dotted effect and yet small enough to be workable. Whatever pattern or arrangement of beds is decided upon, the garden should be symmetrical for the best effect and the pathways need to be sufficiently distinguishable. Perhaps in addition some theme can be followed — a physic garden, a cook's garden, dye plants, *pot pourri* plants, strewing herbs or a nosegay plot.

BELOW *Tile-like squares, each planted with a different herb, make a dainty arrangement for a restricted area. Confine each herb sufficiently to allow it to be reached from the surrounding pathway. If the planted area is to be an island bed, then the taller plants need to be set towards the centre.*

ABOVE *When space is limited, a level site can be formed into a wheel garden with rim and spokes of brick, tiles or wood. Or make a rainbow wheel: red, monarda; orange, marigold; yellow, tansy; green, lemon balm; blue, borage; indigo, basil 'Dark Opal'; violet, peppermint.*

Culinary
Hedge
Lovage
Fennel
Savory
Caraway
Parsley
Sorrel
Thyme
Mint
Lavender

Lavender
Lungwort
Foxglove
Licorice
Yarrow
Feverfew
Poppy
Self
Heal
Monkshood
Physic
Hedge

Germander

C O B B L E S

Chamomile
Turf
Chamomile
Turf

Chamomile
Turf
Chamomile
Turf

Lily
of
the
Valley
Marjoram
Pepper-
mint
Germander
Germander
Thyme
Lemon
Balm
Evening
Primrose
Lavender
Hedge
Solomon's
Seal
Iris
Apple
Mint
Dill
Poke
Weed
Bronze
Fennel
Motherwort
Comfrey
Chives
Chervil
Physic
Hedge
Lavender
Culinary

ABOVE *Pretty and sweet scented, this small formal garden is planned
to provide for a succession of culinary and physic plants. The
surrounding lavender hedge forms the essential part of the integral
design and it will take two or three years to become established.
Space has been created at the centre by keeping the levels low —
chamomile lawn and low germander edging; then the plants rise
irregularly to the four corners. The whole is embraced by the low
lavender hedge; seen across a lawn or yard the herbs can be enjoyed
at a distance, every bit as much as within the garden itself.*

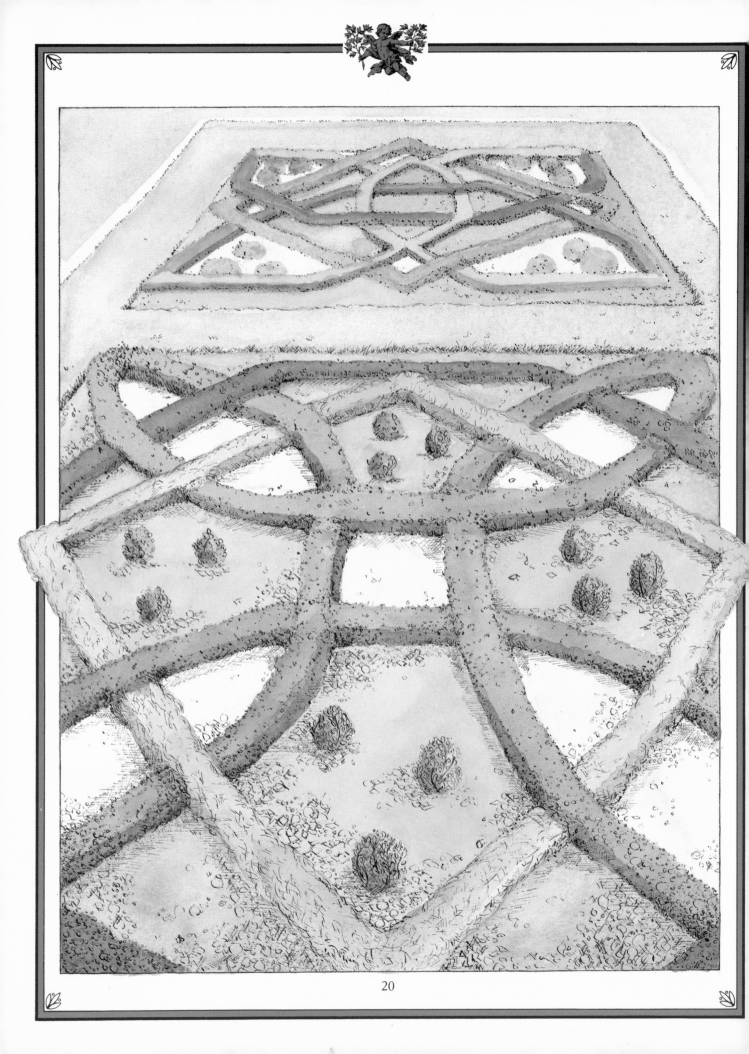

OPPOSITE *Choose compact low-growing herbs to make a design for the knot garden on the left. Although it appears complicated and intricate, only three kinds of herb are used, say hyssop, germander and box. (Thyme, santolina or lavender would be suitable also.) Plant them evenly and very close together to form ribbons. Once they are growing, clip them regularly to achieve a crisp uniform pattern, taking care to create an interlaced effect. Use coloured stones to fill the spaces.*

KNOT GARDENS

The most elaborately-designed formal gardens are made along the lines of the Elizabethan knot gardens, based upon some intricate pattern of beds and interlaced clipped outlines. The design is symmetrical and usually repetitive and is always seen at its best from higher levels of the surrounding garden or from a building.

Old gardening books often contain designs for knots; sixteenth- and seventeenth-century architecture and costume illustrations may suggest designs, Look for inspiration on ceilings, door panels and badges, and transfer them to the ground. In Tudor gardens the knots were probably composed of plants not all of which are today considered to be herbs. Low-growing plants such as marjoram, hyssop, thyme, germander, santolina and box were used to form the threads and outline of the design, and were close-clipped to maintain a crispness of presentation. Box was soon found to be one of the most successful, and today is most commonly employed as the formal edging to many herb beds in both kitchen gardens and decorative gardens. In forming knots, the aim is to plant the herbs close together in chains and to encourage them to develop evenly to the same height; too much unevenness is rather unattractive. Once established, the ribbons of growth need to be clipped with hand shears. The spaces between the ribbons or chains can be filled with coloured shale or pebbles (as was the practice in Tudor England), or they may be filled with a low-growing young plant.

ABOVE *Many garden writers of the 17th century suggested designs for knots. This design from Blake's* The Complete Gardener's Practice *(1656) would not be too difficult to achieve. In practice, decorated tiles (TOP) could suggest ideas for simple knot design. Limit the number of kinds of herb to three or four at the most.*

RIGHT *Part of a simple knot garden in the making. Chains of box and germander, interwoven, once established will be close slipped to make the pattern crisp.*

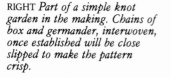

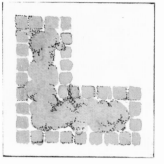

GROWING HERBS IN CONFINED SPACES

Many gardens do not have areas appropriate for herb cultivation, perhaps because they lack light or shelter, or have a very heavy or sticky soil. Most herbs and aromatic plants can be perfectly successfully cultivated in containers — window boxes, troughs, decorative pots or boxes. Suitable compost can be provided and the containers moved around or replenished regularly. A good trick is to sink pots with herb plants into the containers themselves and cover the pot rim with peat or pea gravel over the surface of the larger container. If a plant fails, or grows unattractive as the season progresses, its tiny pot can simply be removed and replaced with something else, and the gravel surface smoothed over as if nothing had happened. Instant gardening!

Rooted cuttings, or the little herb plants that can be bought in markets, should be tucked quite thickly into the larger containers and treated in the same way. Be prepared to change and replace plants that outgrow their allotted space or begin to grow awkwardly and spoil the effect. Remember that especially during warm weather, containers of all kinds need constant attention, particularly watering. Balconies, porches and window-sills for office workers all provide perfectly suitable places in which to grow herbs in an assortment of containers, provided that sufficient light is available. Almost all plants need a minimum of five to six hours of good light at some time during the day.

The word 'container' can be interpreted in the widest sense and can be applied to raised beds, or the tops of walls that surround, say, a patio. When plants are cultivated at waist level the aged and infirm can also participate in gardening; if the raised beds are arranged thoughtfully, wheelchairs can be manoeuvred between them and the invalid can be a herb gardener too.

TOP *A terracotta strawberry jar planted with artemisias and sage.* ABOVE *Herbs tumble from an 18th-century lead water tank to create a miniature herb garden.*

OPPOSITE *A knot garden in the making (see previous page) looks somewhat sinewy in the early stages, but fills out remarkably quickly.*

TOP, ABOVE, BELOW *Specially built raised beds of brick or stone add a decorative dimension to the patio or yard. Herbs cultivated in this way, perhaps mixed in with other aromatic plants bring the aromas nearer to nose level. A seat set in the side invites lingering.*

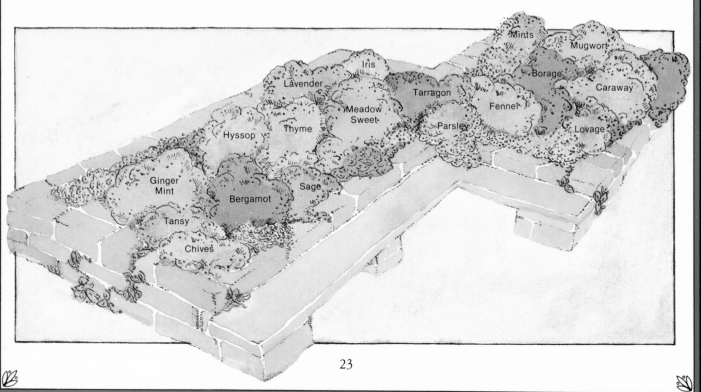

GROWING HERBS IN GRAVEL

Cultivating herbs in gravel gardens is becoming increasingly popular and has the great advantage of being labour saving. Choose good clean gravel or aggregate, or where available, washed stone chippings.

Relatively small areas can be turned into attractive herb gardens in this way. The area must be cleared of perennial weeds, forked over and levelled, then covered with stout black plastic sheeting. Cut holes in this wherever herbs are to be planted, and if young plants are not ready to plant out, push a stake or label into the soil beneath to indicate the position for later planting. Spread the gravel over the whole of the sheeting to a minimum depth of 3 inches, and rake it level. The sheeting will act as both weed barrier and mulch, retaining moisture in the soil. Drainage will only be a disadvantage in wet summers or where large areas have been covered.

A spray over the plants with water in the evening will suffice in all but the warmest of regions. Such a spray played over the whole area, plants and gravel, will heighten the perfume in the garden as the moisture evaporates.

OPPOSITE LEFT *A simple container may be used as the central feature in a small herb garden, and height added by growing fennel in it.*
OPPOSITE RIGHT *Sweet bay is a favourite plant to grow in containers, but needs to be protected from winter winds. It makes a delightful evergreen decoration for a porch or garden room or sheltered balcony.*

Thyme

Iris

Lemon Balm

Borage

Sorrel

Purple Sage

Chives

Apple Mint

TOP, ABOVE *Gravel makes good clean path material, needing little maintenance other than an occasional rake over to keep it neat and level. The whole area can be covered with gravel right up to the plants, to make a small area appear larger. Spread black plastic sheeting over the ground beneath the gravel to prevent weeds from growing through.*

Harvesting

HE growing season for herbs is a comparatively short one, and the period during which the essential oils are at their richest even shorter. So the whole object of herb growing can be jeopardized if the harvesting and drying are not carried out properly. It is essential to know which part of the herb is required — seed, root, leaf or the whole herb — and the time to gather it for best results. Sometimes the timing is critical. In general, leaves are richest in the essential oils just as the flowers begin to open; seeds have to be ripe but need to be caught before the plant sheds them; roots also have to be mature and 'ripe'. The correct time to collect each plant varies from garden to garden and season to season, and can be learned only by constant attention to detail and a little practical experience. Some sprigs of herbs may be picked for immediate use, fresh, like chives, mint, and parsley, whenever there are growing leaves available through the year.

For the amateur herb-grower, two factors are of primary importance. Firstly, never collect more plant material than can be handled in the time and space available, and secondly, only harvest when the plants are dry. This is best done when the heavy dews have dispersed and before the heat of the day; often a gentle shake early in the morning will rid them of dew quite quickly as the temperature rises.

The object of drying herbs is to eliminate the water content of the plant quickly and, at the same time, retain the essential oils. Therefore it is sensible to harvest one plant quite separately from another and to do it in small quantities at a time. Plant material in baskets, boxes, or on sheets — however it is collected — soon wilts, warms up and begins to deteriorate. Deal with a small amount at a time and then return to the garden for more.

RIGHT *Rose heads cut from the plant just as they reach maturity are collected in a box or basket to avoid bruising the petals. Select and handle unblemished flowers with care and do not leave them together in the basket for longer than it takes to collect them, as they will begin to warm up and deteriorate.*

OPPOSITE *The ideal time to harvest herbs is after the morning dew has gone, but before the day becomes too warm. Here, thyme is being cut and collected in a clean dry garden trug. Always harvest healthy herbs when they are in the peak of condition and therefore richest in essential oils.*

ABOVE *Seed needs to be ripe before harvesting. Examine the heads closely to be sure that all the seeds are ready. Here fennel is being inspected.*

ABOVE *Herbs are dry when they are papery to the touch and snap cleanly between the fingers. Remove the stalks and rub down as soon as possible; store immediately in air-tight containers and label with the name of the herb and the date.*

LEAVES

Unless a crop is being cleared, pick a few whole shoots from each plant so as not to jeopardize the plant's continued existence. Cut, rather than pull, them off cleanly and select only healthy insect- and disease-free shoots. Keep the shoots of one plant separate from those of another, even when, say, two kinds of mint are being harvested.

ROOTS

Most herb roots are plump and ripe for lifting in the autumn (fall) at the end of the growing season when they are richest in stored food. In general, iris, elecampane, and aconite are ready in early autumn (fall); sea holly, Solomon's seal, valerian in the spring, and marsh mallow a little later. Lift whole roots with a garden fork or flat-tined potato fork, taking care not to puncture or bruise the outer skin. Rub or wash them free of soil, cut back any residual top growth and fibrous rootlets, cut them into convenient sections or slices and then set them out to dry.

SEEDS

When seed is being saved for sowing it should be allowed to ripen on the plant and be collected only from well-grown, healthy plants. A muslin or thin paper bag popped over the whole inflorescence and secured with a plastic tie or rubber band will contain the seeds as they are released by the plant. Seed being saved for propagation needs to be stored in envelopes of aluminium foil (made by folding foil about the seeds) or in small boxes with a secure lid, and labelled with their name and date of collection.

Where seeds such as caraway, sweet Cicely or dill are destined for culinary use the old flowering stems, or even the whole plant, can be pulled up. By hanging them upside-down in a shaded dry place the seeds will loosen of their own accord and can be collected in paper or cotton bags tied over the flower heads. Alternatively they can be allowed to fall on to sheets of clean paper or cloth beneath. If the latter method is undertaken,

particular care has to be exercised to keep the seeds of different plant species separate.

Holidays frequently coincide with seed ripening, so by covering flower heads with paper bags many seeds can be saved. Once ripe and collected, the seeds need to be separated from the chaff either by simple winnowing, or by sieving, or hand picking. In practice, tilting and shaking them on a sheet of kitchen paper is a slow but sure way of getting the job done.

WHOLE HERB

It may be necessary to cut all the parts of a plant which are above ground, especially if the crop has been grown for harvesting. Parsley can be cut at any time when the plant is not in flower and fresh green leaves are available. Others need to be cut before the flowers bloom but after the leaves and shoots have reached their full size. Again, the same rules apply regarding keeping the plants separate and dealing with a limited amount of material at any one time.

BARK

Bark is usually shaved off branches in the autumn (fall) and is then dried. The active elements vary in quantity according to season; homeopathic medicine, for example, stipulates at what time of year bark should be cut. It is important not to leave large patches of bare wood when shaving bark off; it is better to prune away whole branches and strip bark from them.

FLOWERS

Flowers are harvested mainly for their colour, shape and decorative attributes, and are used to embellish food and drink. Pick them just as they become perfectly formed, and avoid bruising and crushing the petals. Gather a few at a time on a baking tray or plate on which they can be separated with as little handling as possible. Lavender flowers gathered for lavender bags and rose buds for inclusion in *pot pourri* need to be picked while immature in order to retain their shape and scent.

Some flowers may harbour earwigs or other insects; these can be floated out by dipping the flowers in water before using them. Whatever use the flowers are to be put to, it is important to deal with them immediately after picking. Flowers for crystallizing ought to be fresh or else they will fold together. Those for freezing can be quickly blanched in tiny bunches in boiling water, popped into a freezer bag, labelled and dated, and put into the freezer. Alternatively, a favourite mixture of herbs can be frozen together in bags in small quantities, so that they are ready for use without waste.

Large soft leaves, such as basil, should be oiled on each side — a good olive or sunflower oil will do — flattened between sheets of waxed or greaseproof paper, and then frozen. Another method is to put tiny sprigs of, for example, mint, marjoram, lemon balm or thyme into the ice tray with water and freeze them in cubes. Herbs such as mint and borage can be chopped then frozen in cubes; single borage flowers set in ice cubes can be popped into drinks at a later date.

ABOVE *Pull apart the petals of harvested roses for quick and even drying, but leave a few buds intact to decorate* pot pourri. *Roses destined for inclusion in* pot pourri *are best dried together with other flowers, to help form a homogenous mixture where all the scents combine to make a rich fragrance.*

Drying

O herb can be stored fresh. Much of the value and flavour of a herb can be lost by ineffective drying; if the properties and colour of the herb are to be preserved, the whole drying process must be carried out as quickly and evenly as possible. Shade, air and warmth are the essential requirements — constant temperature being the critical factor.

Herbs (grown and) dried at home, with a little care, can be far superior to most commercially available products. However, not all herbs dry equally satisfactorily — chives and fennel, for example, simply flop.

The simplest drying method is to tie each kind of herb separately into bunches. Each bunch should be tied loosely by the stems to allow air to circulate and left hanging freely. Hang them in a dry shaded place — attic, spare room, summer house, clean garden shed or barn. In drier warmer climates, bunches of herbs can be hung out of doors in the shade, or in the high ceilings of a warm room with the windows open, or even in a bedroom where a breeze can be circulated through louvred shutters. This method of drying is difficult to control and the end results are unpredictable.

RIGHT *The freshly harvested sprigs of rosemary in the basket will soon be spread to dry on airing trays. Finally they will be stored in air-tight jars.*

OPPOSITE *Seed heads can be laid sparingly over newspaper to dry. Once ripe, the seed will fall on to the paper and can be retained. Here fennel is drying.*

CONTROLLED DRYING

Quicker and more consistent results can be obtained by spreading sprigs of herbs evenly over trays, box lids or drying frames, or merely on to a table on sheets of paper. Keep the sprays of one kind of herb together and separate from the others. Sprigs are the easiest to handle — only large-leaved herbs like lovage and comfrey need to have their stripped stems removed before drying.

Drying frames should be made from some light porous material such as muslin or fine netting stretched over a rectangular wooden frame to allow air to circulate. The herbs need to be turned over by hand several times during the first two days.

Trays can be put into an airing cupboard or domestic boiler room and the doors left open. In England, the domestic Aga or Rayburn cookers provide the perfect herb-drying conditions — the herbs can be placed on racks above or in the slow oven with the door left open. The plate-warming compartment of a domestic cooker is another possibility and perhaps gives best results for drying flowers like chamomile. Again the door should be left open to allow the water to evaporate.

ARTIFICIAL HEAT

For better results the drying process needs to be speeded up and controlled. Some artificial heating needs to be provided capable of mantaining an equable temperature, and some ventilation to keep the air moving. For the first 24 hours a temperature of about 32°C/90°F needs to be maintained to reduce the water content as quickly as possible. The temperature can then be reduced to around 25°C/75°F to complete the process. The whole process takes from three to six days if properly carried out.

Microwave ovens are more problematical as it is very easy to overdry and cook the leaves, which sadly results in their complete disintegration. Two or three minutes are sufficient for drying.

Herb leaves are properly dried when they snap easily between the fingers and thumb. Some stems are slow to dry, so the dried leaves can be stripped off and stored and the stems abandoned. If herbs are stored before drying is complete, moisture will be reabsorbed from the atmosphere and the material will soon deteriorate.

DRYING ROOMS

Where a considerable quantity of herbs are to be dried, or when dried herbs are being prepared for a market, it is worth considering creating a special drying cabinet.

The correct drying temperature must be achieved before the fresh herbs are taken in; and perhaps an extractor fan set high in the room will be needed to keep the air moving. The warmer the air, the more moisture it can hold and this needs to be removed. An extractor fan set high in the room will both remove the moisture and keep the air moving. The moisture content of most plants is above 70 per cent and the object of brisk drying is to change the condition of the leaf rather than its chemical content.

Trays can be fitted into specially constructed racks. If freshly

OPPOSITE LEFT *A modest harvest of herbs drying in small bunches on the floor of a summer house. Warm spare rooms, garden sheds, barns — any space that is clean and dry can be used to dry household quantities of herbs.*

gathered material has to be brought into the room where other herbs are still drying, the moisture drawn from the fresh material will be reabsorbed by the dry herbs. The trays of fresh herbs should therefore be placed high up in the room nearest the extractor fan.

RUBBING DOWN

Once the herbs have cooled down after drying, the rubbing down process can begin. This is best carried out in a well ventilated place, wearing gloves and a smog mask (if any quantity of material is to be handled.) Hand pick the leaves from the stalks. Some, like marjoram, can be stripped simply by running the fingers along the stem. Discard the stalks and crush the leaves either in a domestic grinder or with a rolling pin or simply by rolling them up one kind at a time in a cloth and rubbing the cloth.

STORING

Once rubbed down, dried herbs need to be stored immediately in air-tight, dark containers to prevent them from picking up moisture again from the air. Glass jars are ideal if they are to be kept in a dark cupboard — nothing will destroy the quality of a herb quicker at this stage, than exposure to light. Label the jars immediately with the name of the herb. Most domestic herb requirements are comparatively small; there is little point in storing them for posterity! It is better to keep just enough for the ensuing winter's needs.

At this stage, at the end of a busy week and a summer of cultivation, the amount of dried herb looks rather small and perhaps unrewarding. The finished product may weigh only an eighth of the original fresh weight, but nonetheless it retains all its aroma and essence.

BELOW *Collect a few pretty sprigs of herbs and leaves in summer to press and preserve for winter gifts. Their beauty and aroma can be used to decorate cards, bookmarks and letter heads, and bring memories of summer herb gardens.*

CULINARY HERBS

Culinary Herbs

MANY culinary traditions relying on herbs originated in the ancient world and reached northern Europe, including Britain, with the Romans. Forgotten during the Dark Ages, herbs were reintroduced into cultivation by the monks in the early Middle Ages and were the main flavouring, colouring and preserving agents. Even when the great spice markets of London flourished, herbs were cultivated, marketed and used in homes as very important items for the still room. Only the nineteenth-century industrial revolution brought a decline in their popularity with the mass production of synthetic flavourings.

Since the Second World War there has been a marked reawakening of interest in herbs and natural foods, which was initiated in America. When herbs are grown well the nutritional, digestive and preserving values are retained.

In the past, on both sides of the Atlantic, culinary herbs and vegetables were grown together in the kitchen garden. But twentieth-century gardeners have developed a love for decorative herb gardens, where 'sweet' herbs grow alongside 'pot' herbs and where numerous plants that had almost been forgotten have been brought back into cultivation.

All cooks have their own ideas about which herbs to use, but some herbs have an almost classical affinity with certain foods — these are listed in the following catalogue of culinary herbs. Often a small bunch of several sprigs of different herbs may be added to a dish, by tying them with cotton and allowing the bunch to float in the pan or dish during cooking time, and then removing it before serving. Chopped fresh herbs can be added to salads or sauces, or mixed into cream cheeses, or even be incorporated into herb butters. Vinegars may be flavoured with herbs, or in some instances coloured by them — chive flowers for example, turn vinegar a pretty pink.

OPPOSITE *A selection of culinary herbs: tarragon, borage, allium and parsley.*

ALEXANDERS

Smyrnium olusatrum (Umbelliferae) B

A somewhat unfashionable pot herb that grows wild in southern and western coastal areas of the British Isles, but in cultivation is a hefty, handsome plant, particularly in spring before most other herbs are ready for use. (In America, the name alexanders sometimes refers to the indigenous wild angelica, a far taller and more elegant plant.)

Alexanders, black lovage, black pot herb — call it what you will — gives a good celery/parsley flavour to soups and stews. Alternatively, the young leaves can be shredded and included in coleslaws. The white-green flowers are fragrant, the leaves large, smooth, shining and deeply divided, becoming rather tough to eat later in the season. But, for early summer interest in the garden, the great burgeoning shoots are lush and pale, the stout furrowed stems quickly reaching 0.9-1.2 m (3-4 ft). An ancient pot herb, replaced by celery for the modern palate.

CULTIVATION Seed may be saved and sown, but it is available from specialist seedsmen. Sow mid- to late-summer in an open position, to produce appetizing leaves the following spring. It is from the black 'twin' seed that the plant takes its name of black pot herb, the seed being used to flavour stews.

ANGELICA

Angelica archangelica (Umbelliferae) B

An imposing and dramatic plant which, given good growing conditions, attains 2 m (6½ ft) in height, with large green-white mophead flowers held aloft. A good plant for the back of a border (especially when protected from rough winds) because the stout green ribbed stems stand up for themselves and hold the glossy green leaves about them like flounces.

Strictly speaking, angelica is a biennial plant, forming a good clump of foliage the first summer and dramatic flowers the second, dying after the seed has set. But by cutting back the growth in autumn (fall) and preventing the flower heads from seeding, the plant can be maintained as a short-lived perennial.

Angelica is cultivated mainly for its green stems which can be candied and used in confectionery. A chunk or two cut at flowering time makes a good addition to stewed fruit, or it can be used in jam-making as a substitute, especially for rhubarb. However, every part of angelica is useful. The dried root (when infused) makes a stimulating tonic reputed to encourage a dislike for alcohol. The ground roots are used for sachets, and an oil derived from the root is used in liqueurs. The juniper-flavoured seed can be substituted for real juniper berries in the making of gin. Leaves are edible as a vegetable when cooked and served with butter, offering a spinach-like flavour. In the past angelica was recommended for a wide range of ailments, and legend tells us that in medieval times an angel 'visited' a monk, directing him to use this plant to alleviate the sufferings of victims of a plague — hence the specific name *archangelica*.

CULTIVATION Angelica seed loses its viability so it is important to sow the seed when fresh. If this cannot be done, store it in a fridge or ice box throughout the winter, and then sow in the spring in tiny pinches, thinning out all but the best plants once germination has taken place. The seedlings do not transplant well, but it is worth trying when they are very small. Plant out at least 90 cms (3 ft) apart to allow the plants to develop uninhibited. A good rich loam ensures the most marvellous of all herb garden plants, otherwise growth will be restricted and poor in colour. Angelica dislikes hot, humid climates and appreciates a spot in gardens where it can be in the shade for some part of every day.

BASIL/SWEET BASIL

Ocymum basilicum (Labiatae) A

An ancient plant from the Pacific Islands which reached England via Asia and Europe in the sixteenth century, and was taken by early settlers to America.

A tender herb, several types of which are in cultivation. The large leaved, common or sweet basil, *Ocymum basilicum*, is the plant to choose for the kitchen with its strong, spicy, clove-like aroma. Dwarf or bush basil, *O. mimimum*, is hardier but has a weaker flavour.

Sweet basil bears tiny, white, purple-tinged flowers in midsummer and juicy aromatic leaves. It reaches 50 cms (1½ ft) in height. 'Dark Opal' has a gingery aroma, and when used shredded in salads adds a decorative air and exotic flavour. 'Dark Opal' was developed in 1962 at the University of Connecticut, and represents something of a breakthrough in herb cultivation, because, almost exclusively, herbs have escaped the attentions of the hybridist. Moreover, it was awarded the All-America medal by the seedsmen.

CULTIVATION In zones with a cold winter, sow basil in early to mid-spring in boxes or in frames, or later out of doors when all danger of frost has passed. The best results are obtained by starting off the seedlings with protection and maintaining a high temperature until they can be hardened off and planted out safely.

In warmer zones, sow directly into the beds, and thin out to about 20 cms (8 ins) apart, or transplant. Basil seedlings transplant easily. A plant can be potted up and kept indoors to maintain a fresh supply of leaves until late autumn, or it can be grown indoors where the plant will get at least five hours of sunshine each day. It is a good patio or window-box plant, and a happy inhabitant of a sunbaked yard.

BAY/SWEET BAY

Laurus nobilis (Lauraceae) P

Bay, or sweet bay (the latter name being preferred in America) is a highly esteemed inhabitant of the herb garden. In classical times heroes and poets were adorned with garlands of bay leaves. The Latin name of the plant is honoured to this day in the title Poet Laureate.

Of Mediterranean origin, the bay is an evergreen tree. It is usually grown as a bush, and it hates cold winds. For this reason alone it has come to be cultivated habitually in large containers, its branches trimmed to some formal shape. It decorates porches, yards and balconies, and can be moved into shelter if necessary in the winter.

In warmer districts it is a good plant to grow as the surrounding hedge to the herb garden. The height and shape of the hedge, or of individual bushes, can be controlled by clipping or pruning. Bright green smooth oval leaves, punctuated by lovely fluffy-faced beige-yellow flowers at midsummer, make the bay easy to identify. (It is vital not to confuse it with cherry laurel — *Prunus lauroceracus* — which produces prussic acid.

In the kitchen a crushed leaf of bay added to prepared meats, stuffings, casseroles and chowders is almost traditional, and it is one of the vital ingredients of bouquet garni, the others being parsley and thyme. A few sprigs cut just before the flowers bloom, tied together and hung in a warm, dust-free place will provide dried leaves of bay for culinary flavouring. Bay is one of the very few herbs which is not used fresh as the flavour would be far too pungent.

CULTIVATION Cuttings taken with a heel in early summer (when the new spring growth has hardened a little) and made about 10-15 cms (4-6 ins) long are the most reliable method of propagation. Insert them in pans or pots, potting up separately once the roots are established, and keep them thus for a year or so before planting out. (Layering of established plants in summer is an alternative method of propagation.) Once plants are growing well, an occasional spray with water helps to keep the leaves clean and shining.

B I S T O R T

Polygonum bistorta (Polygonaceae) P

Snakeroot is another vernacular name for bistort, and it is descriptive of the stout contorted rhizomes which are rich in tannin and for which the plant is well known. Because of its appearance, it is also called snakeweed. The name bistort refers to the twice twisted rhizome which helps to make the plant such good ground-cover in the decorative herb garden, where it is a handsome plant.

Upstanding, oval, bright green leaves folded at the midribs surround military straight stems bearing sugar pink, occasionally white, flowers in fat spikes up to 50 cms (1¾ ft) during the summer. It is a native European plant with a long history of medicinal use due to its astringent properties, the black skinned roots being rich in tannic acid.

In northern England bistort has served the country people as 'Easter Ledges', the leaves forming the main ingredient of Easter or bistort pudding. Combined with the early leaves of nettle, parsley and blackcurrant and mixed with barley and oatmeal and bound with egg and butter, it used to be the main course in an iron-rich nourishing meal. Try young leaves shredded and added to salads.

CULTIVATION Bistort is happy in any good garden soil in either sun or shade, and is a generally undemanding plant. Propagation is by seed or by division at planting time, or in the autumn (fall) from established plants. The form to use in the decorative herb garden is *P. b.* 'Superbum'.

BORAGE

Borago officinalis (Boraginaceae) A

Believed to have originated in the Aleppo area of Syria, borage is now happily at home as a cultivated plant (and occasionally garden escape) far from its native land. 'Burradge' appears on the seed order, 1631, of John Winthrop Jr, so it was by then considered to be a necessary herb by the settlers. Irrevocably associated with courage and cheerfulness, it is reputed to 'drive away all sadness'. Both leaves and flowers are rich in potassium and calcium, and are therefore a good blood purifier and tonic.

The entire plant is covered in soft, bristle-like hairs, which in dew or moonlight endow the plant with a halo. It is one of the most delightfully decorative plants of the herb border, especially when it stands up straight, but unfortunately most plants have a tendency to loll about! Plant them on a bank or terrace, or even in the top of a wall, so that the swinging inflorescences can be seen from below. On average 60 cms (2 ft) high and having pale-green juicy stems, borage is a branched plant with little sprays of flowers at the end of each branch. The star-like flowers are a deep-blue (with an occasional pink one) and they are never all in flower at the same time. However, there is always something in bloom from midsummer until the autumn (fall) frosts arrive.

The leaves have a cucumber flavour, and once chopped the hairiness disappears. Use them young and fresh as borage does not dry well. The pretty flowers make a delightful decoration to fruit cups, fruit compôtes and salads and may be frozen in cubes or crystallized (thereby preserving their strong colour). Older and larger leaves may be boiled and served with butter or a sprinkling of caraway seed, or they can be dipped in batter and served as fritters.

To treat bruises on the body, pulp fresh leaves and bind into position to reduce the swelling and inner bleeding.

CULTIVATION When borage is happy it will self-seed all over the garden, and the seedlings will survive provided that a really severe winter does not follow. It is considered to be a hardy annual in all areas except the very coldest, and seed is sown afresh each spring. Seed can be sown *in situ*, or even started earlier inboxes, although it is difficult in some areas to transplant unless the seedlings are planted out when very small. Leave 45 cms (1½ ft) between the plants so that their spreading stems do not become entangled. Borage thrives in a sunny situation and well drained light soil, and will grow in pots or window boxes. A seed or two sown in autumn (fall) in a pot indoors will provide fresh leaves throughout the winter, but need lots of light to thrive.

CARAWAY

Carum carvi (Umbelliferae) B

Caraway perpetuates itself in the garden by self-sown seed, ensuring a filmy greenness among the herbs. The leaves are thread-like and bright green; the stems are smooth, reach 60 cms (2 ft) in height and support dainty heads of purple-white flowers in high summer. These are followed by the familiar black, ribbed seeds used to flavour confectionery, cookies, bread and liqueurs (especially Kümmel).

A herb of ancient cultivation, legend endows it with the power to prevent lovers and doves from straying. It was thus a popular ingredient of love potions in medieval times and was fed to doves, pigeons and poultry to prevent them from wandering.

To harvest the seed, cut the flower head once the seed is ripe (and before it scatters) and either hang the heads up in a paper bag or folded in a clean cloth. This way the seed can fall naturally when it is fully ripe. Sieve out any pieces of stalk and store in an airtight container. One common practice is to scald the freshly collected seed with boiling water to rid it of insects which can then be dried off in the sun before storing.

CULTIVATION Seedlings do not transplant well, so sow *in situ* in spring or autumn (fall). Caraway thrives in all but the most humid warm regions, and does best from fall-sown seed because the germination is quicker from fresh seed. Subsequently the little plants need to be thinned so that they are about 15 cms (6 ins) apart, and may be grown in either groups or rows. But, when they are grown for their carrot-like roots it is best to do so in rows and treat them as a vegetable. They will grow in almost any well drained soil but need plenty of sun to produce seed of an acceptable flavour.

CHIVES

Allium schoenoprasum (Liliaceae) P

Chives (sometimes known as onion chives) are one of the most widely grown herbs. They resemble trim tufts of grass and are thus ideal for use as a path edging for both the kitchen garden and herb garden. As they mature the leaves become circular and hollow, and reach about 30-40 cms (12-15 ins) in length. (Giant chives grow a little taller). Their precise habit makes them excellent material for cultivation in pots for yards and balconies, or in window-boxes where good drainage can be assured.

The flavour is refined and onion-like and is best before the plants flower, or in plants that are prevented from flowering. When chopped as a garnish for cheese and egg dishes, soups, salads, sandwiches and quiches, the grass-like strips are added fresh just prior to serving. Chives are rarely used in cooking as the mild flavour is extinguished.

Chinese chives or garlic chives (*Allium tuberosum*) form clumps in the same manner as onion chives, the only difference being that the grass-like leaves are flat. The flavour is pleasant and nearer to garlic. They grow up to 60 cms (2ft) tall with upstanding, mauve-pink flower heads all summer. Both flowers and leaves may be incorporated in salads and herb butters.

CULTIVATION Divide established clumps of bulbs every three years in the spring, and transplant clusters from the outer edges of the clumps. Alternatively, chives can be raised afresh from seed. Although they thrive in any good garden loam, they show a marked preference for slightly acid soil and need to be kept moist throughout the growing season. Choose a place where they can enjoy some shade during the day and remove the flower heads to maintain a continuous supply of flavoursome leaves. The foliage dies down in the winter, so cover a plant or two with dry leaves to encourage a few early spikes for their fresh flavour. Alternatively, pot up a clump of bulblets in the autumn (fall) to keep in a porch or on the apartment windowsill for fresh early spikes. In those regions where the summer temperature remains above 32°C (90°F) clumps can be planted out afresh in the autumn (fall) to provide a winter supply of leaves.

In the garden allow at least two or three plants to flower for the sheer beauty of the purple-pink bobbed heads. Float these as a garnish in soups — especially consommé — or use them to decorate the cheese board or cold collations.

CORIANDER

Coriandrum sativum (Umbelliferae) A

The rounded beige seeds of coriander are best known as a flavouring for pickles and curries in both Europe and America. But in India and the Far East green coriander — or the fresh foliage — accounts for the distinctive curry flavours. This foliage happily is now becoming a market vegetable commodity much more widely available. In Indian cooking the seed is roasted before being ground for use.

A native of southern Europe and the Middle East, coriander used to be a popular herb in England up to Tudor times. The early settlers in America included coriander seed among the beloved items they took to the New World, as did the Spaniards in Mexico.

Today, coriander enjoys a wide popularity. However, among certain groups it still has mythical associations — the Chinese believe it to be endowed with the power of immortality and Jews include it in the bitter herbs prepared for the Feast of Passover. Today its unique flavour is being rediscovered. For the best flavour, seed should be freshly ground before use, when its slightly orange flavour lends itself to inclusion in breads, cookies and pastries.

The entire plant makes a decorative addition to the herb border — it may also be cultivated in pots quite successfully — and will reach a height of 45 cms (1½ ft). The lower leaves are fan-like (a distinguishing feature), the upper ones filigreed and the tiny flowers in high summer are a pinkish mauve. Before the seed ripens the entire plant can be distinctly odorous, but on maturity the rich aroma develops.

Sprigs can be frozen or preserved in salt and oil; coriander does not dry successfully.

CULTIVATION Coriander grows best in a dry atmosphere — in fact it is difficult to grow in damp or humid areas, and needs a good dry summer at the very least if a reasonable crop is to be obtained. Choose a sunny place and sow seed *in situ* once all danger of frost has passed. Alternatively, sow into decorative containers and continue to cultivate as a container plant on an apartment balcony, sunny patio or yard. The stems are weak and the plants tend to loll about and appear top heavy, so either add a twiggy stake or give it a companion to lean against!

DILL

Anethum graveolens (Umbelliferae) A

A native of the Mediterranean countries and Russia, dill has plumes of finely cut blue-green leaves and acid yellow flowers in flattish heads in mid summer. It grows to about 90 cms (3 ft) in height. However, the hollow stalks, when top heavy with flowers, can easily be knocked over by the wind, so it is advisable to try and find a sheltered spot for growing dill. Its reputation as a soothing herb is supported by the fact that both leaves and seeds contain a mild sedative, although the flavours vary considerably. Dill water was a remedy for restive infants 100 years ago and dill is still the sweet-tasting ingredient of the proprietary gripe water.

Its main use in the kitchen is as an addition to pickled cucumbers and gherkins; in America these are known as dill pickles. Dill vinegar is another popular condiment, made by macerating half a cup of dill seed in a quart of malt vinegar for three or four hours, then straining off the liquid and bottling. In central and eastern Europe chopped dill leaves are often used to garnish a dish of boiled potatoes or soured cream sauces, lending them a flavour which is nearer to parsley or anise than the sourness of the dill seed.

For the richest flavour harvest the leaves just before the plant flowers. Small sprigs wrapped in foil and sealed will keep for several weeks in the freezer. Alternatively, chop the leaves, add a little water and freeze in ice cubes.

CULTIVATION Sow seeds in a sunny spot, then thin the seedlings out so that they are about 20 cms (8 ins) apart. They resent being transplanted, and show their displeasure by bolting into flower prematurely. Sow in the spring as soon as the ground is warm, and follow with small sowings at fortnightly intervals throughout the summer to maintain a good supply of fresh leaves. Where winters are very mild seed can be sown in the autumn (fall) to overwinter and provide a good early crop the following spring, or self-sown seedlings will overwinter. Never sow near to fennel, as the two plants tend to cross and the subsequent seed is not as flavoursome as might be expected. The filmy foliage may be cut about six weeks after sowing and the seed collected when fully ripe.

FENNEL

Foeniculum vulgare (Umbelliferae) P

A superbly graceful and tall plant, fennel is easily recognized by its finely cut foliage which can be harvested and used fresh throughout the summer. It is far too sappy to dry. A mediterranean plant grown and used in northern Europe since Roman times, it was taken to America by the settlers for the digestive qualities of its seeds. They provide an anise-flavoured condiment which allays hunger and were used in Europe to mitigate the effects of Church-imposed fasts. More recently in American Puritan communities, seeds of fennel and dill were taken to church to nibble during long services and were known as 'meetin' seeds'.

Fennel is a traditional seasoning for fat meats like pork and, used with restraint, it makes a good accompaniment to poultry and lamb. It is delicious on herring and other oily fish, or to flavour yoghurt as a salad or vegetable dressing. Sometimes the seed is used to flavour bread.

Collect the seed heads just as they change colour and hang them up in a dry, airy, shaded place where the curved, ridged seed can fall onto paper or cloth beneath to be collected. The thick, glossy main stem reaches some 1.5 m (5 ft) in height with feathery soft, ferny foliage topped by dainty heads of yellow flowers in umbels, which bloom in midsummer. The Romans held fennel in high regard as a panacea for several ailments, and as the bestower of power and safe passage. In the Middle Ages in Europe it was sometimes stuffed into keyholes to stop the passage of evil spirits.

CULTIVATION Fennel is a tall plant suitable for the back of the herb border. Seed should be sown in the late spring. To maintain a continuous supply of fresh leaves throughout the season, sow a few seeds in succession with about a 10-day interval between sowings. It can be grown as an annual, although the established roots make good plants that overwinter easily. Divide such established roots in the autumn after the seed has been harvested.

H O P

Humulus lupulus (Cannabinaceae) P

An easily recognized twining plant, hop scrambles up hedges and posts quite naturally in both Europe and America. Known universally as the most important ingredient in the brewing of beers, it is the dangling cone-like, green female flowers that are used. (The tiny male flowers are on separate plants.) Having slightly narcotic properties they are habitually used to pack herb pillows which purportedly soothe insomniacs, or, when warmed, help to relieve earache. The papery buds can be eaten, although they should be blanched first to remove the bitterness which is caused by lupulin, which is an oily substance. Hop tea is a generally soothing herbal tea or tonic, considered to aid digestion.

A splendid plant to introduce into a sunny herb garden where there is well-worked soil. The plants grow in a clockwise fashion and should be trained onto a post, trellis or wall, where they make an attractive screen. A bine can grow as high as 6 m (20 ft), with its flexible and fibrous stems. A lovely patio or deck plant, the broad vine-like leaves are one of the main attractions of the plant.

Lupulin is one of the most effective vegetable bitters available. Hop bitters can be made by mixing equal quantities of angelica stem and holy thistle with an equivalent weight of hop flowers. Many country beers included hops for their bitter flavour.

CULTIVATION Seed is obtainable from specialist seedsmen — or established plants can be divided. It takes about three years before good flowers are produced, and the bines need to be cut back to the ground each autumn (fall). It is not generally necessary to tie the plants; if good support is provided the plant will gradually wrap itself around it.

LEMON BALM

Melissa officinalis (Labiatae) P

Lemon balm is a cottage garden plant which is grown for its lemon-scented leaves. It is also cultivated as one of the strewing herbs for its clean pervading fragrance.

It forms a dense round bush about 60-90 cms (2-3 ft) high, and as much across. In warmer climates it can reach 1 m (4 ft) in height. In its best forms the leaves are variegated with clear yellow; all forms dry well and are suitable for inclusion in *pot pourri* recipes.

In the kitchen, dried crushed leaves can be added to stuffings for poultry and meat; flower tips and young leaves can be floated in wine or fruit cups and may be used as a substitute for lemon juice in jam-making. Balm was the principal ingredient of *eau des carmes*, distilled by the Carmelite monks in seventeenth-century Paris as the forerunner of *eau de cologne*.

CULTIVATION Although slow to germinate, seed is otherwise easy to grow, and as it is so fine it hardly needs covering. A quicker method of propagation is to take cuttings in late spring and plant them out once they are established in warm districts, or in the following spring. A moist soil in a sunny spot enhances the essential oil of this plant, ridding it of the slightly musty overtones that develop during dry seasons or on light, dry soils. It is especially good, in both appearance and aroma, in the controlled conditions of containers. Cut back to soil level in the autumn (fall) to encourage young fresh growth and good fragrance.

Lemon balm is happiest in moderately warm regions, where it grows a little more lushly but it does not like great humidity and needs a cold winter to give of its best.

LOVAGE

Levisticum officinale (Umbelliferae) P

The lovely healthy green leaves, hollow stems and sulphur yellow flowers of lovage are a lush addition to the herb garden. A vigorous handsome plant, it can reach 90-150 cms (3-5 ft) in height and responds to good cultivation. It dies down each winter.

A native of the Mediterranean it is perhaps one of the less easily recognized herbs today, but it was known in the early monastic gardens as a physic plant and was used as an antiseptic and deodorant for suppurating wounds. As a pot herb lovage's earthy, nutty flavour provides a substitute for celery in casseroles and soups and comes into its own in vegetarian cookery because, unlike celery, the chopped leaves and tubular stems retain their full flavour in cooking.

Ripe seed can be harvested just before it is about to fall by cutting the flower heads and drying them off over clean paper or cloth indoors. The aromatic oblong seeds are easily stored and may be used for flavouring bread and pastries or for sprinkling on boiled rice.

CULTIVATION Lovage is one of the few herbs tolerant to shade; it seems to adapt to both full sun or partial shade with impunity. It will reward good cultural care by lasting for several years, when the root stock becomes stout and woody and can be used as a casserole vegetable after the bitter-tasting skin has been removed.

It will grow in most places where it gets the period of dormancy which is necessary to complete the growth cycle. Sow seed in late summer once it has ripened, either in a pot or *in situ*, and retain only a few of the best seedlings. One or two lovage plants are sufficient for the needs of most families, but more can be grown for garden decoration. Keep the seedlings watered in both autumn (fall) and spring, and take care that the young lovage plants are not allowed to dry out.

MARJORAM

Origanum onites (Labiatae) P

All the marjorams have a warm sweetly pungent aroma. Perhaps that of pot marjoram (*O. onites*) is somewhat rougher, but nevertheless it is one of the most popularly cultivated herbs, and flourishes in temperate climes. Its flowers are pink and white in high summer, and it forms good clumps of growth up to 60 cms (2 ft) in height.

The three kinds included here are the subject of some confusion, probably because until the 1940s common marjoram (*O. vulgare*), a red-stemmed perennial which spreads by tiny rhizomes, was called wild marjoram in American cookbooks. Today it is known as oregano. (Further confusion arises because in some countries, notably Mexico and the southern states of America, oregano is the colloquial name for totally unrelated plants with a similar flavour.)

Sweet or knotted marjoram (*O. majorana*) is a tender plant from north Africa which, in June, has mauve flowers almost hidden in knot-like clusters of leaves in little 'blobs' at the stem tips — hence the name knotted marjoram. It provides by far the best flavour for cooking. Except in hot climates, it is treated as a half hardy annual, producing bushy little plants about 20 cms (8 ins) high. An excellent herb to accompany meat (especially cold prepared meat) and bland vegetables like courgettes and potatoes.

All the marjorams dry well for winter use, and both flowers and leaves ought to be incorporated in *pot pourri*.

CULTIVATION Pot or wild marjoram is simple to raise from seed sown in spring or from summer cuttings or from root division in autumn (fall). On the other hand sweet marjoram needs to be treated as a half hardy annual. All three kinds can be started by sowing indoors or in cold frames early in spring, and are ready to transfer out of doors as soon as the temperature gets up to about 7°C(45°F). In very mild zones they can be treated as hardy.

Origanum dictamnus, dittany of Crete is grown as oregano in America, often as a pot plant and usually only for decoration — although its leaves can be added to salads.

M I N T

Mentha species (Labiatae) P

Numerous mint species are grown almost everywhere, some wild, some cultivated forms, and all bearing a variety of vernacular and catalogue names which leads, inevitably, to some confusion. A further complication arises because the mints themselves hybridize and can vary in appearance according to environmental factors. But by examination of the essential oils, using chromatography, the identification and relationship of the whole range of mints has been made possible. But, as with all herbs, the country names persist.

Spearmint, the classic ingredient in mint juleps, was recorded as growing in Plymouth, Mass. in the early 1600s by Elder William Brewster. It appears, also, in Josselyn's seed list but is absent from the Winthrop seed order of 1631, for the simple reason that it was available locally and did not need to be imported. Mints have only one purpose in life — to walk about the plot and propagate themselves.

The kitchen garden mints are the most widely grown. Spearmint or garden mint (*Mentha spicata*, formerly *Mentha viridis*) used in the traditional English mint sauce to accompany roast lamb, is perhaps the commonest, with narrow pointed leaves, growing anything from 30-90 cms (1-3 ft tall). If left to flower in midsummer, it grows purple spikes, held well above the leaves. Apple mint (*M. rotundifolia*) has large, round, soft, rather downy leaves and, if left to flower, pink spikes growing up to 1 m (3¼ ft) high. The cream, variegated form with leaves bordered and overlaid with cream and young shoots often entirely cream is *M. rotundifolia variegata*, and is usually called pineapple mint. It is a good decorative garden plant often retaining its attractive foliage throughout the summer. Ginger mint or scotch mint (*M. gentilis*) is another decorative leaved plant, especially good in its *variegata* form when the golden variegation of the rather pointed leaves and its military trimness, often up to 40 cms (1½ ft) high, add greatly to the herb border. Raripila or pea mint (*M. raripila rubra*) with dark red stems and dark green rounded leaves with red-purple midribs, provides the most exquisite flavour.

All the foregoing are good culinary mints but the largest plant is Bowles's mint (*M. × villosa*) and its *alopecuroides* form is without doubt the connoisseurs' culinary mint. It is a vigorous plant, growing up to 1.5 m (5 ft) high, with broad leaves smeared with pale woolly down. The hairs disappear upon chopping or pounding.

Of the mints used in confectionery and the preparation of pharmaceutical products, peppermint (*M. × piperita*) is the most widely used. Two varieties, black and white, grow to about 1 m (3¼ ft), the former with black-purple stems and both produce a sharp clean oil. In the kitchen peppermint can be used to flavour fruit cups, sweets and puddings and to make a tisane from the dried or fresh leaves.

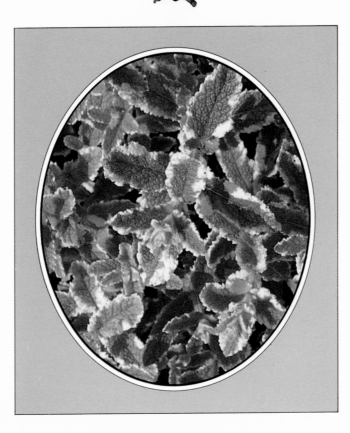

M I N T *CONTINUED*

Mentha species (Labiatae) P

The range of scent and flavour present in mints is a consequence of the barely perceptible variations in composition of the essential oils which can occur within a genus. A whole scale of scent is provided by the same oil; the minute chemical variations between one species and another are themselves affected by time of season, soil and weather — all contributing to the various overtones. Thus we can find mint described as gingery, lemony or peppery. Explore these slight variations in flavour by adding finely chopped mint just before serving to starters such as grapefruit or melon, or to citrus fruit desserts and chocolate mousse.

The smallest leaves of any of our cultivated plants belong to a mint, the Corsican mint (*M. requienii*). Unlike all other mints, this one seeds itself when it is well grown and provides ground cover. It is slightly peppermint scented, but is not a culinary mint.

The soft leaves of the mint are difficult to dry well — they tend to blacken and soon shatter. Try not to collect too many shoots at any one time unless the whole plant is being sacrificed. All mints can be included in *pot pourri*, especially the fruit-scented ones. Little sachets of dried leaves can be stored in cupboards and if rubbed occasionally will emit their aroma afresh.

CULTIVATION Mint is propagated by planting pieces of the rooted stem — known in Britain as Irishman's cuttings — about 5 cms (2 ins) deep in moist loamy soil, at almost any time during the growing season. Apple mint, sometimes called dryland mint in America, will tolerate less moist soil; they all like the sunlight. The plants need to be confined to their allotted space and this is best achieved by encircling the area with bricks or tiles, or pushing plastic strips into the ground to prevent their advance.

Container growing is possible provided regular watering can be assured — otherwise the containers need to be sunk into the ground. All mints can be grown indoors (although they tend to become scraggy) except for apple mint which sometimes makes quite a handsome plant.

A productive mint bed in the herb or kitchen garden should be remade and moved every three or four years to reduce the likelihood of mint rust disease.

Crowns of mint plants can be boxed or potted up in winter and taken to a warm greenhouse or conservatory to force succulent fresh shoots which become available within three or four weeks.

PARSLEY

Petroselinum crispum (Umbelliferae) B

All forms of parsley are grown as annuals, although strictly speaking they are biennial plants. By removing the flower heads the productive life of the plants can be extended and the quality of the foliage flavour maintained. The most familiar ones are the nicely curled-leaved sort (called French curly-leaved parsley in America) beloved of fishmongers as a garnish. The plain-leaved kind, *P. neapolitanum* called Italian plain-leaved parsley in America, has a more pronouced flavour and is preferred by some cooks, especially for long slow cooking. Nibble a sprig or two of this iron- and vitamin-rich plant to discover the refreshing flavour. It ought not to be known merely as the universal garnish and ingredient of parsley sauce for it has too fine a flavour. It is an ingredient of bouquet garni, sauce verte and sauce tartare. Parsley tea is a tonic and diuretic.

Hamburg parsley, *P. c.* 'Tuberosum' is a variety with plain unfrizzed leaves grown for its root which is used as a winter vegetable.

CULTIVATION Originating from the regions around the Black Sea, parsley is best sown in mid to late spring as an edging in the kitchen or herb garden or even to a flower border. Germination can be unbelievably slow, about six to eight weeks is the norm, but to encourage it try soaking the seed overnight and wetting the drill with water trickled from a kettle of boiling water immediately prior to sowing. (Legend has it that parsley seed goes nine times to the devil and back before germinating.) Subsequently thin the little plants with care during showery weather, or remove alternate plants for use until they are left standing about 30 cms (1 ft) apart. In all but the most northerly parts of America parsley can be sown in early spring, or even in the autumn (fall) before the ground freezes. Remove the flower stalks as they form to keep the plant buoyant and the leaves full of flavour.

Grow some in a container and keep it in a porch or on the kitchen window-sill for a fresh supply of leaves during the winter months, as parsley does not dry successfully. Although it will freeze, it loses its pert frilliness and is no longer attractive as a garnish.

PURSLANE

Portulaca oleracea (Portulacaceae) B

One of the plants taken as seed from England and other European countries to America by the settlers; the older leaves provided a green vegetable, the stems were pickled as a relish. A rather sprawling succulent annual with tiny yellow flowers and reddish stems which try to stand to a height of 15 cms (6 ins). For salads and sandwiches the sharp clean flavour mixes well with other leaf crops and is useful in coleslaws — the flowers scattered on top to decorate the dish.

A leaf or two held under the tongue is said to allay thirst and Culpeper recommended it as garden purslane, 'so well known that it needeth no description' and said it was a remedy for numerous ailments — all of which suggest it to be soothing and antibiotic.

CULTIVATION Sow seed in late spring when all fear of frost has passed, preferably in a sandy light soil and a sunny position. Thin seedlings out so that they are 10 cms (4 ins) apart, or try it in a window-box where good drainage can be provided. Purslane rewards quickly; leaves can be picked within six weeks of sowing.

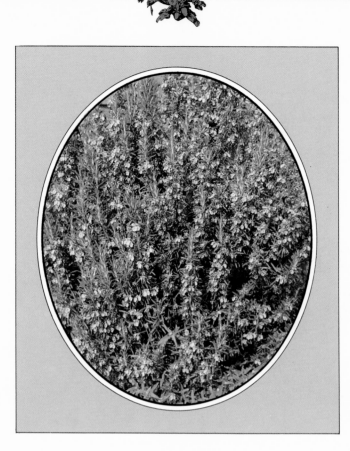

ROSEMARY

Rosmarinus officinalis (Labiatae) P

A very popular shrub with richly resinous evergreen foliage, which needs only to be brushed by the hand to release its fragrance, rosemary is said to be for remembrance. Its wonderful powder blue flowers bloom inter- mittently very early in mild localities until early summer when they enshroud the entire shrub. In happy circumstances it will rise to 1.6 m (8 ft). Culpeper recommended more than a dozen uses for rosemary and said 'The Flowers and Conserve made of them, are singular good comfort to the Heart.' Rosemary used to be burned in chambers to freshen the air; included in herbal tobacco; used in body cosmetics for its deodorant properties; included in *pot pourri*; and used in the treatment of many inner bodily complaints and as an external antiseptic and embrocation.

As a culinary herb its flavour is pronounced, so exercise restraint in its use. Because the leaves are spiky, remove them before serving the dish. It is at its best as a flavouring for lamb or as a marinade ingredient for strong game.

CULTIVATION Take cuttings of the twisted wood of non-flowering shoots in early summer, or layer established branches in summer. Choose a sheltered position and well drained soil in which to plant it so that it can sunbathe. Where winters are cold, grow rosemary in containers that can be taken into shelter. The thick growth tolerates clipping, so it can be controlled.

SAGE

Salvia officinalis (Labiatae) P

There are several forms of the common or garden sage; all are reasonably hardy and keep their leaves in winter. In America leaves can even be harvested during the winter in the southern states, and we know from physic receipts that it was grown there for medicinal purposes in the seventeenth century.

The broad-leaved kind rarely produces its mauve flowers and is the best plant to use for its culinary purposes because the essential oil is rich. But for herb garden decoration use the purple-leaved or red sage (*S. o. purpurea*) and a daintier form, painted sage (*S. o. tricolor*), in which the young leaves are haphazardly splashed with cream, pale green and cherry pink; this is a less hardy plant. The narrow-leaved sage (*S. hispanica*) and the narrow-leaved golden sage (*S. icterina*) are all useful substitutes — the latter the sweetest and best of all for stuffings to accompany delicate meats. The whole range of flavours and aromas can vary even further when plants are cultivated on different soils and it is worth experimenting to find a plant that provides the most acceptable flavour, devoid of bitterness. Move it about the garden or try rooted cuttings elsewhere until the best flavour is produced. Sage tea made from fresh or dried leaves and flavoured with lemon juice has been used in the past in many forms as a headache remedy. Cold sage beer or ale is said to dispel depression.

Lax bushes of *Salvia officinalis* grow about 40-90 cms (1½-3ft) high and as much across, and ought to be replaced every four years or so, although many serve a useful life for much longer. Harvest sprays and hang them up in bunches to dry any time during the spring and summer. Once dry there is no fear of sage leaves reabsorbing atmospheric moisture, but nevertheless, store in containers.

Sage is supposedly the herb of eternal youth and is used in stuffings, cheeses, kebabs, leek pie and with gammon. Alternately, it can be used as a dentifrice, gargle and mouthwash, and when burnt as a deodoriser for animal and cooking smells.

CULTIVATION Select a sunny corner and alkaline soil for sage is a native of the Mediterranean shores and flourishes best when it is warm. Propagation is from summer cuttings taken with a heel or by layering established branches in spring and autumn (fall). Seed is unreliable and it rarely sets in Britain because sage is reluctant to flower. Where seed is available it is a slow and challenging method of perpetuating the plants. Keep the bushy plants well pruned to encourage young shoots with a strong flavour and because sage has a strong tendency to become leggy and twiggy.

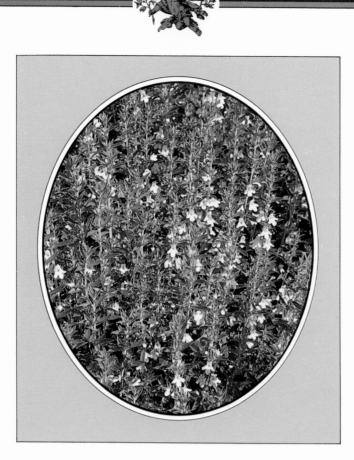

SAVORY

Satureia species (Labiatae) A & P

There are several *Satureia* species all of which have pungent flavoured small leaves and are natives of southern Europe. The two most commonly cultivated are summer savory (*S. hortensis*) and winter savory (*S. montana*) and both were known in America by 1631 when John Winthrop Jr purchased seed, because both are mentioned as 'sauory'. Both have been flavouring herbs for centuries, strong enough to mask putrefaction and useful to add to bland tasting pulses, especially broad beans.

Summer savory is an annual plant growing about 30 cms (1 ft) high at the most, with tiny narrow leaves speckled with oil glands, and spattered with dainty pale lilac flowers which bloom intermittently lending a speckled look to the entire group of plants.

Winter savory is an evergreen perennial more commonly grown and perhaps a little more rough and peppery in flavour, but not markedly so if the plant is kept well clipped to ensure a succession of young shoots. Winter savory makes neat lilac flowers about 30-40 cms (1-1½ ft) high and has tiny pale lilac flowers if allowed to flower. In places where the winters are mild winter savory makes a pretty little low-growing hedging plant; elsewhere it needs some winter protection during the prolonged frosts.

Use fresh leaves where possible to avoid any staleness. Sprinkle on soups or vegetables (particularly broad beans) to bring out their flavours. In fact both savories provide a good condiment with poultry, eggs or fish. Mix some with cider or wine vinegar intended for vinaigrette.

CULTIVATION Sow summer savory seed in spring in drills, and thin the little plants to about 5 cms (6 ins) apart. Propagated winter savory from cuttings taken in spring may be divided at any time and the same applies to roots. Seed can be tried, but it is annoyingly slow to germinate and does not always produce alert-looking seedlings. Both need their share of sunlight and good drainage, as do all plants that come from the Mediterranean. Winter savory can be grown in boxes or containers and can then be brought indoors for protection during the winter, or even kept indoors where the shoots need to be constantly pinched back to prevent it from becoming leggy and scrawny. It certainly needs good light during the winter when grown in this way.

SEA HOLLY

Eryngium maritimum (Umbelliferae) P

At first sight the uninitiated might take sea holly for a thistle: it is a spiny plant with rather undulating leaves, each curve ending in a fearsome spine. It is nevertheless a handsome plant and offers a welcome variation among the other herb garden umbellifers.

A native of the shorelines of Europe where the large root can penetrate beyond shingle to water, it is a cultivated form that is grown in gardens. The stems burst from the upper part of the stem — the joint surrounded by spiked leaves powdered with a silver bloom — and produce hard conical flower heads, each frilled like a posy with spiny purplish bracts.

The aromatic roots used to be boiled and roasted to produce a flavour reminiscent of chestnuts, and crystallized as comfits or sweetmeats and called 'eryngo' or 'eryngo root'. Gerard gave elaborate instructions for preparing the roots and claims them to be 'exceeding good to be given to old and aged people that are consumed and withered with age, and who want natural moisture'. Today, eryngo root is added to jams, jellies, compôtes, and is also candied as a sweetmeat. The young flowering shoots may be boiled and eaten like asparagus — the prickles disappear in cooking.

An indigenous American eryngo, *E. aquaticum*, is employed in physic as an expectorant and tonic, and not as a sweetmeat.

CULTIVATION Sea holly is easy to grow in good garden soil in a sunny position, but to provide good strong roots it is necessary to provide sharp drainage so that they are encouraged to grow in search of water. Seed is available from specialist seedsmen. Root cuttings can also be tried for propagation, or the plants can be divided carefully in the spring. Avoid all moisture around the collar of the plants. They grow least happily in very warm humid regions.

SORREL

Rumex acetosa (Polygonaceae) P treated as A

The sorrel of herb gardens is a superior broad-leaved form of the wild plant native to the temperate regions of the Northern Hemisphere, including Britain and America. Distinguishable by the succulent leaves up to 10 cms (4 ins) in width, the upper ones with downward pointing lobes, it is known also as garden or broad-leaved sorrel and can reach 1 m (3¼ ft) high.

The main culinary attribute is the tangy flavour of the leaves, which is at its most refined just before the spikes of rusty pink flowers appear — so remove the flower buds to maintain a supply of tender leaves. It is useful for tenderizing meat: just wrap it around the steak, or add it pounded to the marinade. Alternatively, use it as a substitute for vine leaves, enfolding risotto mixtures. The French make sorrel soup from both sorts of sorrel.

CULTIVATION Raise new plants each season for the most refined flavour, sowing seed in spring in moist well-nourished soil where there is some shade during the day. Set in drills as for most salad crops; thin the little plants to about 30 cms (1 ft) apart. Prevent bolting by removing flower buds and pick the leaves frequently to maintain a supply of fresh succulent leaves.

Pinch out the flower heads to prevent flowering and seeding, or else be prepared to remove self-sown seedlings before they develop. Once sorrel establishes itself the roots plunge deeply and are difficult to eradicate. In really warm summers, or generally warm regions, sorrel leaves tend to become bitter. A mulch around the plants will help to keep the soil cooler, but once the season cools down the leaf flavour will improve.

S WEET C ICELY

Myrrhis odorata (Umbelliferae) P

Another of the tall-growing umbelliferous plants that inhabit herb gardens, sweet Cicely is distinguishable by the sweet licorice-like aroma of both foliage and seed. A tall feathery plant with lacy soft-textured green leaves flecked with white, and tiny white flowers in late spring which are followed by long ribbed seeds. These talon-like seed heads become quite dramatic when ripe with glossy bronzed seeds.

A truly attractive plant which lives up to its name and reaches about 1 m (3¼ ft) in height. It is one of the first plants in the herb garden to produce new growth in the spring.

The leaves do not dry or freeze, but the seed is strongly aromatic and stores well. Chop the leaves or seeds when green for inclusion in salads or to decorate dessert mousses and ice cream. As a sweetener the leaves are useful in fruit compôtes (especially for a diabetic diet) or with acid flavours like gooseberries or rhubarb. The tasty roots serve as a vegetable, eaten either hot with a bland sauce or cold in salad dressed with vinaigrette.

CULTIVATION The long carrot-like roots love a cool moist soil, and given partial shade the plants will survive for several years. However, it is best to divide them in the autumn (fall) when the top growth dies down. Plant out any self-sown seedlings which may emerge all around the mother plants. Purchased seed should be sown in the autumn (fall).

Sweet Cicely is not suitable for growing in humid areas, because it needs a good dormant period during the winter to produce its root and lush foliage.

An American woodland plant, *Osmorrhiza longistylis*, known as smoother sweet Cicely, is very similar but has a very slightly larger leaf. The roots used to be nibbled by children for the anise/licorice flavour.

TARRAGON/FRENCH TARRAGON

Artemisia dracunculus (Compositae) P

The true French tarragon or estragon is a superior herb, sometimes difficult to grow and reluctant to flower in the damp climates. It seems happiest in warm areas, but is difficult to grow in conditions that are both warm and humid.

With spiky bright green leaves and an upright stature, growing 70 cms (2½ feet) tall, tarragon produces little underground runners that creep about the garden. It is perhaps the most superior culinary herb, with a blunt flavour that adds a bite and enhances all other flavours.

Tarragon vinegar is made by steeping the fresh herb in wine vinegar for six to eight weeks, shaking the bottle occasionally. Sprigs to be used in this way ought to be picked early in the season when the essential oils are rich. A superb flavour to add to egg dishes, try to use the herb fresh as the flavour becomes stale when dried. It is better to quick-freeze tarragon to capture its wonderful flavour.

Russian tarragon (*A. dracunculoides*) has an inferior flavour, and is not generally recommended for culinary purposes.

CULTIVATION A plant for the sunniest driest places, tarragon is a lover of warmth and good drainage. The top growth needs to be cut back early in the autumn (fall). In colder parts it needs to be protected in some way to help it through the winter. Dry bracken or leaves or a peat mulch covered with plastic is usually sufficient, but in more extreme conditions apply the mulch after the ground has frozen solid, using dry straw or salt hay.

Try to pot up a young plant to grow indoors and keep through the winter. It will need a place where it gets whatever sunshine is available. Tarragon is not easy to keep in this way, so do not be too disheartened if it decides to go — nothing will persuade it to remain! Propagation is from root division or stem cuttings — seed offered is usually that of Russian tarragon.

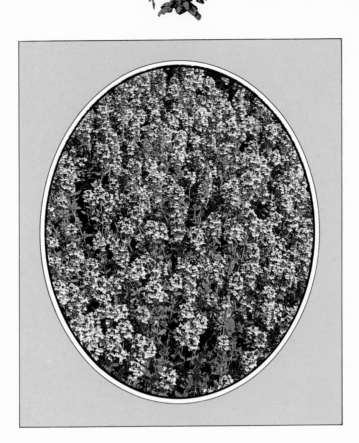

THYME

Thymus species (Labiatae) P

Thyme is one of the most important culinary herbs, and is used for its essential oil called thymol, which is a preservative. Garden thyme (*T. vulgaris*) is the main one grown for culinary purposes, although others offer variations of the true thyme aroma. Among the many decorative sorts are lemon thyme (*T.* × *citriodorus*) and caraway thyme (*T. herba-barona*) and one or two others, which are best used mixed with garden thyme. The nuances of flavour displayed among the thymes are not as varied as those of the mints, but the range is useful in cooking.

Garden thyme forms a cushion-like mound of growth; all the other thymes form a carpet-like growth covering the ground. Where the decorative value of a 'flowing' edge is needed, do not plant *T. vulgaris*, but select one of the others. A little hummock of garden thyme will reach about 30 cms (1 ft) in height and its cultivars are about the same size. The carpet-forming sorts are ground hugging and are no higher than 5-8 cms (2-3 ins).

Harvest thyme for drying before the plants flower and hang up to dry in a warm shaded place or lie the sprigs on a cloth or paper in a warm place.

Thyme has a powerful aroma and may be successfully dried or frozen. It is an ingredient of bouquet garni and always needs to be used with restraint as its overpowering strength can survive the longest cooking, and can become dominant. However, this lasting quality can be used to advantage in slowly simmered rich game dishes.

Its many uses include terrines, cooked meats and sausages, and as a preservative and flavouring in stews, vegetable broths, cream soups and stuffings. The lemony aroma of lemon thyme is a good accompaniment to fish dishes and makes an interesting addition to tea-breads and some desserts.

CULTIVATION Choose the sunniest part of the garden where the soil is well drained or even dry, and a little limy. Most plants will be either short-lived or need some protection from the cold and dampness in winter. In the drier and warmer maritime regions where winter temperatures do not fall too low or too quickly, it is always worth trying to keep thyme. It is a good plant for troughs and containers which can be brought indoors during the winter for protection.

Propagation is from seed sown in spring, and the tiny plants put out once they are big enough to handle at about 5 cm (1 in) intervals. Otherwise, take tip cuttings in summer before flowering starts.

WILD STRAWBERRY

Fragaria vesca (Rosaceae) P

A native of light woodland and grassy banks throughout the temperate regions of the Northern Hemisphere, the true wild strawberry provides deliciously sweet deep red fruits at midsummer — that is, if the birds can be kept away from them! In Tudor times English physicians used the wild strawberry as a cleansing tonic, and Culpeper recommends them for external use to clear blemishes and skin burns. They have been used also as a dentifrice. By 1629 the Virginian strawberry, (*F. virginiana*) had crossed the Atlantic to Britain and Parkinson was writing about it in his *Paradisius*. Its lusciousness had been discovered by early settlers at Point Comfort, Virginia.

Before that in England the wood strawberry and the long-stemmed or *hautbois* strawberries were cultivated to adorn tables, both as decoration and as sweetmeats. Water the wild strawberry well at flowering time to enjoy its pretty fruits in fruit salads, compotes or as decoration for cheesecakes or rich cold meats. It is regarded as a weed in many prim gardens, but it can be attractive if left to run about among paving stones and in dry walls, or to edge a path in kitchen or herb gardens.

CULTIVATION One tiny daughter plant is all that is required. Plant it in a sunny spot where the roots can be kept cool by stones of some sort. The real trick is knowing how to restrain its progeny from wandering across the garden.

Specialist seedsmen offer seed, which should be sown in pots or boxes in spring and planted out as tiny plants. But it may also be cultivated in pots or window-boxes where a cool root run can be provided. Replace the mother plant each autumn (fall) for the best results. A lovely plant for children to grow, or for invalids to enjoy planted in a window-box.

EALING

HERBS

Healing Herbs

HE medicinal value of plants is governed by their chemical composition, or active principle. From ancient cultures an intimate association has existed between man and his healing plants; botany and medicine stemming from very much the same source. The value of most of the physic plants used today must have been confirmed by trial and error over many centuries and varying cultures. Modern concepts relating to healing plants started in Europe in the sixteenth century with the printing of herbals, themselves based on the codices and practices of the classical world. Between those two cultures lay centuries when the use of physic plants became irrevocably linked with magic, emblems and superstitions. Primitive societies held curious ideas in which lay the origins of the folklore that surrounds the herbs today.

The sixteenth-century European medical schools were the first to establish botanic gardens, which were for the study of living plants. There are now more than 400 such gardens throughout the world, many of which conduct continuous research into medicinal plants.

In 1585 Raleigh organized the first colonizing expedition to the New World accompanied by men qualified to record the natural history of Virginia. There then began a great exchange of plants between the New World and Europe. Into Virginia came the plants Europe had cultivated and used for centuries, fruit, vegetables and more importantly, herbs — herbs for sustenance and herbs for healing.

OPPOSITE *The healing herbs section of the Acorn Bank herb garden.*

Individual herbs are not the best plants for garden decoration and for this reason they are always more effective when assembled together.

Various attractive schemes can be devised to enhance their decorative values. In this island bed, the central diamonds contain comfrey, licorice, motherwort and foxglove, plants of medium height, and they are surrounded by lower-growing plants such as pulmonaria, yarrow and pennyroyal. Consideration has also been given to the overall colour effect, so that a blue-mauve-pink theme emerges, supported by dusty grey and blue green. Repetition of a planting theme is always a positive approach to garden design, never more so than for herbs. Where space allows, these taller diamond shapes among the lower-growing herbs could be repeated.

Variations on the colour of the diamonds could be introduced, for example yellows, with tansy, evening primroses, variegated lemon balm and fennel, with ginger mint; golden marjoram and variegated thyme would look pretty among the surrounding smaller plants.

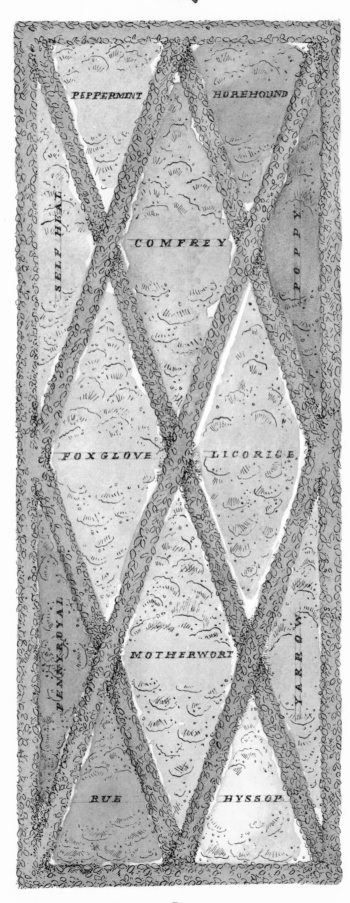

PEPPERMINT   HOREHOUND

SELF HEAL   COMFREY   POPPY

FOXGLOVE   LICORISE

PENNYROYAL   MOTHERWORT   YARROW

RUE   HYSSOP

AMERICAN MANDRAKE

Podophyllum peltatum (Saxifragaceae) P

A plant of shaded meadows and damp woodland indigenous to the Atlantic regions of America, mandrake, mayweed or wild lemon arrived in England c 1664. The drug obtained from the fleshy fibrous root was known to the American Indians as an emetic and vermifuge, and has a powerful and beneficial action on the liver, but must be used only in competent hands.

In English gardens it is seen as a semi-aquatic plant often incorporated in the decorative garden, but invaluable in the spacious bog/herb garden. Underground stems have many branches which are matted together with long fibrous runners. There are two kinds of stem, one bearing a single leaf, the other two leaves and a single white flower. Ultimately the plant attains 45 cms (1½ ft) in height, but it flowers early in the year before this height is reached. The leaves are broadly hand-shaped, roughly 30 cms (1 ft) across, rounded and deeply veined, and assume a deep, rich, red colour in late summer. The scented flower is followed by a large seed capsule which turns yellowish or red on maturity. Although the leaves and roots are poisonous this capsule — a fruit — is edible although somewhat acid in flavour.

CULTIVATION Divide established clumps in spring and plant in moist, humus-rich soil in a partially shaded spot. Twelve seeds form in each berry and may be sown when ripe. Where they are happy the plants spread once established, but the underground stems can be easily pulled apart.

BELLADONNA

Atropa belladonna (Solanaceae) P

When the great English herbals were written in the sixteenth and seventeenth centuries, belladonna or deadly nightshade apparently grew quite plentifully in the English countryside in chalk and limestone districts. Today, it is a very rare native perennial and is cultivated in specialist collections and botanical gardens. Culpeper treated it with some suspicion for when describing nightshade, presumably *Solanum nigrum*, he says, 'Have a Care you mistake not the Deadly Nightshade for this; if you know it not, you may let them both alone, and take no Harm having other Medicines sufficient in this Book'. Belladonna is also cultivated in America.

Deadly nightshade or dwale, as Chaucer knew it, is a powerful narcotic and holds a lurid fascination. Long known for its highly poisonous qualities, it is nevertheless still used in medicine, especially homeopathic medicine, for which it is farmed in eastern Europe. Belladonna is reputed to be the name allotted when the juice was used by Italian ladies to lend greater brilliance to their eyes by dilating the pupils. The smallest drop put into the eyes externally had the desired effect. When taken internally the narcotic powers induce sleep, loss of voice, fevers and a racing pulse. Various proprietary preparations have included belladonna for external use as plasters and as poultices for injured joints and bunions. It must be used only under reliable medical supervision. In the garden the plant ought not to be handled when there are cuts or abrasions on the hands.

Belladonna grows from a thick branching root to a height of 150 cms (5 ft) with a somewhat lax stem, much branched. Large oval pointed leaves grow in pairs and are pale on the underside; it is in the axils of the leaves that the rather sinister, dingy, purple-brown flowers dangle. Attractive cherry-like berries follow (about which children need to be warned), green at first and subsequently turning to a luscious black.

CULTIVATION When belladonna was cultivated commercially, bonfire ash used to be worked into the soil before sowing. But in the garden, provide an alkaline soil in dappled shade. It is a plant well worth adding to the collection of physic plants and although it is perennial, it is best treated as a biennial.

To collect the seed from the black poisonous berries, wear rubber gloves and squash the berries under running water to release the seed. Continue to wash until the water runs clear of the purple juice.

BLACKROOT

Leptandra virginica (Scrophulariaceae) P

North American Indians knew this plant and used it to clear bile and to aid digestion. A native of eastern and southern America, it is known as Culver's root or Culver's physic. Erect stems up to 150-210 cms (5-7 ft) tall bear neat long spikes of white flowers in mid summer, rising above a good whorl of deeply lobed and ponted leaves. Rhizomes, the useful portion of the plant, are dark brown to purplish black and run horizontally just below the soil surface. They contain a volatile oil and when dried are used in the treatment of dysentery, enteritis and allied complaints. When fresh the root itself is an emetic, contradictory perhaps, but proof, if proof were ever needed, that plant drugs are best dealt with by trained herbalists.

CULTIVATION A plant seldom seen in herb collections in England, blackroot is now included in some National Trust gardens and is easy to cultivate. Propagation is by division of rhizomes in spring, setting them just below the soil surface in a well drained position where some organic material has been incorporated. The clumps need to be divided every three or four years. Hardy throughout America, it prefers higher altitudes and some shade.

BLOODROOT

Sanguinaria canadensis (Papaveraceae) P

A spring-flowering perennial, bloodroot is a native of the North American continent from Nova Scotia to Florida and westward to Nebraska. The bark of the root was used by the North American Indians to dye themselves, and the root itself as a narcotic. They taught the colonists to use the plant as a dye plant and as a treatment for congested chests. The orange juice which flows from the bruised plant used to be dropped on to sugar lumps and administered for coughs and colds. The flavour is revoltingly bitter.

A solitary pure white, waxy flower is held on a stem 15-30 cms (6-12 ins) above deeply cleft, large leaves. However, it is the rootstock that is of value: thick, fleshy and rich with deep orange/brown juice. When it is harvested and dried it becomes brittle and almost odourless. There is evidence that it was employed as a treatment for pulmonary consumption and for reducing high blood pressure. External application has been used successfully in cases of ringworm, eczema and ulcers, especially those accompanying broken varicose veins.

CULTIVATION Choose moist rich soil which has been well worked, so that the root can develop. The shade-loving bloodroot needs some sunshine during the day. Propagation is by seed, where this ripens, otherwise by division of rootstock in the autumn (fall), winter in very mild zones. The flowers do not last very long, but the leaves are dramatic enough to decorate a shaded corner in the herb garden.

CANDYTUFT

Iberis amara (Cruciferae) A

A tiny plant native to the British Isles on thin upland chalky soils, candytuft is not very widely cultivated in herb gardens. Tiny scattered pale green leaves are almost submerged by chalk-white flower heads in the cultivated form, which is no more than 15 cms (6 ins) tall. Rounded pods follow and contain an abundance of seed, from which homeopathic herbalists make a tincture.

    All parts of the plant are used, the seeds most of all. They are considered effective against rheumatism and often relieves deep water retention — or what our grandmothers called 'dropsy'.

CULTIVATION Seed is available from specialist seedsmen and must be sown *in situ* in spring once the ground has warmed up. In colder zones it needs to be sown early in boxes or pots and kept under protection until the seedlings can be put outside. They need to be thinned out later so that they are about 5 cms (2 ins) apart. Candytuft is a good plant to use as an edging or to form a ground pattern in decorative herb gardens. It loves the sunshine and needs good drainage on a light alkaline soil. Try it in pots on apartment window-sills where it will get at least six hours of sunshine a day.

COMFREY/COMMON COMFREY

Symphytum officinale (Boraginaceae) P

Comfrey is a plant with a predilection for dampish soils and waste ground near river banks where its black-skinned root can penetrate into the soft earth. It is chiefly for the rich mucilage which it contains that comfrey is prized pharmaceutically. The generic name *Symphytum* is derived from the Greek *symphuo*, meaning to be planted alongside.

Traditionally known as saracen's root, the common comfrey is believed to have been brought back to England by crusaders who had discovered its great therapeutic value in helping tissue to knit together. It served as a major healing herb, and its mucilagenous products were put to use as a bone-setting plaster. The early settlers took it to America and when Josselyn visited New England he declared that 'Compherie' grew well, in his book *New England Rarities Discovered* (1672).

Although the appearance of comfrey is unmistakable, there is a constantly discussed similarity between its young leaves and those of the foxglove. Comfrey has a rough hairiness; the veins of the leaves are closer together and there is a clamminess about it which is absent in foxglove.

The fresh leaves of comfrey form a good poultice or compress for sprained or twisted joints, and need to be wrapped in some sort of cloth as the hairy leaves can cause skin irritation. Dried leaves serve the same purpose but are not easy to dry without shattering. The mashed, sticky, creamy root also provides healing plasters and was used formerly in the relief of pulmonary and throat disorders, and in the healing of stomach ulcers.

Flowers appear in early summer in dangling coxcombs of bells — blue, white, mauve and pink — held on boldly arched stems. Comfrey grows to a height of 80 cms (2½ ft) and the stiff, angular, hollow stalks are covered with rough hairs. Fresh flowers and leaves produce a yellow dye. Contrary to the general rule, comfrey roots are harvested in the spring.

CULTIVATION When grown from seed, the plants are slow to reach maturity. More reliable plants are obtained by root division in spring. Select moisture-retentive soil, or even a poorly drained corner, and comfrey will thrive for many years. Plants have been known to span a generation.

Comfrey thrives happily in all but the very coldest regions where it can be propagated by root cuttings.

ELECAMPANE

Inula helenium (Compositae) P

Formerly generally grown for medicinal purposes, elecampane is a native of northern and central Asia, and is now naturalized — as a garden escape originally — in the whole of Europe. The settlers took it to America for its medicinal properties. It now grows wild from Nova Scotia to Ontario, North Carolina and Missouri and its cultivation is hardy, but it is quite unsuccessful in the southernmost states because of the high humidity and warm winters. A number of handsome elecampanes are cultivated in gardens, but *helenium* is the officinal plant because it concentrates its active principles into its rootstock. The Romans called it *enula campana*, the 'Inula of the fields' — from which elecampane is a corruption.

Shaggy, thin, yellow daisy-like flowers backed by matted hairs are borne singly on 1-m (3¼-ft) stems during the summer. The rough stems are clasped by the leaves, the lower ones quite large and apparently edible as a pot herb. The real value of the herb is in the rootstock which contains a pungent oil that on harvesting smells of ripe bananas and is powerful and warm in flavour. The Romans used it in much the same manner that horse-radish is used today, as well as candied sweetmeat. This idea persisted for centuries and candied, round, sugared slices were sold, coloured with cochineal. The astringent oil provides the antiseptic for the relief of bronchitis and asthma, and its inulin soothes sore throats.

A strong infusion of the leaves used warm is effective in reducing acne and in the treatment of skin eruptions of farm animals — hence the colloquial names scabwort and horse heal.

CULTIVATION In some parts this plant is regarded as a coarse-growing invasive plant, suitable only for rough places. But by ripping back the new growth or dividing the plant frequently after flowering it can be contained in the herb garden.

Propagation is by the offshoots taken from the established clumps when they are being divided or pulled back in the early autumn (fall). Shoots always have little roots on the runners and it is a simple matter to re-establish the plants. They are easily grown and undemanding of soil — however, they prefer a dampish foothold.

E VENING PRIMROSE

Oenothera biennis (Onagraceae) B

The oil of evening primrose is currently attracting considerable attention on both sides of the Atlantic for use in nervous disorders in general, and multiple sclerosis in particular.

It is called evening primrose because it transforms itself from its daytime bedraggled appearance into a fluttering pale yellow beauty in the evening, when its fragrance becomes increasingly powerful. Flowering begins in early summer and continues well into autumn; towards the end of summer the flowers tend to stay open all day. Older country names are moths, moonflower, primrose tree, and in North America, night willow herb.

An indigenous plant of America, extending from Labrador to the Gulf of Mexico and westward to the Rockies and flourishing in thickets and fence corners, it reaches 1.5 m (3½ ft) or more in height. A flat rosette of large pale green leaves develops the first year and the upright stem bearing the rather floppy yellow flowers in succession the following year. Frequently, particularly in America, the flowers are produced in the first summer, seed is set and the plant dies. But once introduced there is always a plentiful supply of fresh seedlings about the herb garden. The stem base is red, and as the leaves die they too assume the same colouring.

Evening primrose is thought to have arrived in Europe via Italy, and certainly as seed in ballast soil in England around 1621. It has become naturalized, particularly on sandy estuaries in the west country, and on sand hills in areas near ports. It is also at home on the dry soils of railway embankments. Now it is also a cultivated plant in gardens where its long flowering season is of value. (Several other species, all of them natives of America, are cultivated in British gardens and some are fragrant and hold their flowers open throughout the day, but *Oenothera biennis* is the true herb.)

The principles extracted from the stem bark and leaves were used for their astringent and sedative properties, and were used for digestive and nervous disorders. Today it is the essential oil that is of importance.

CULTIVATION Choose a dry, well drained soil and dry sunny corner for the best results and sow the seed *in situ* in late spring to produce flowers the following year. Alternatively, sow seed in early spring as soon as the soil warms up after the winter and transplant the seedlings — this will often encourage the little plants to flower the first year. The fleshy roots like to be able to forage, so a good depth of soil will give the best results. Once introduced into the garden, evening primrose will stay.

FOXGLOVE

Digitalis purpurea (Scrophulariaceae) B

No synthetic drug has replaced the cardiac glycosides that are obtainable from the foxglove. It therefore remains of immense importance in medicine and is an essential plant in the physic garden. One of the most poisonous plants of the British flora, it is a true biennial. The rosette of leaves is formed the first year and the flower spike the second; the plant then dies, but usually leaves a clutch of children around it. Occasionally a late-formed rosette may persist for the whole of the second year and flower in the third.

The tongue-shaped foliage is deeply veined, soft and dark green, but the real joy of the plant is in its spire of dangling purple-red bells spotted within, which hang on one side of the spike. It usually grows to 1-2 m (3¼-6½ ft) and flowers in early to mid summer.

A plant of ancient use and certainly recognized by the Anglo-Saxons in England, the value of foxglove in the regulation of heart activity was fully appreciated only in the eighteenth century following the work of Dr William Withering. Although Gerard grew foxglove in his garden it was only administered externally at that time in the treatment of wounds. Gerard quaintly recommends it for those 'who have fallen from high places'. No evidence exists of foxglove having been among the commonplace herbs required by the settlers in America and it is probable that it was not a European import there until its value was established. (Other *Digitalis* species do not contain digitalin.)

CULTIVATION Foxglove is easy to cultivate from seed, and once established there will always be some self-sown seedlings about. Somehow they always thrive best when allowed to select their own standing room, and foxglove has a pretty habit of showering its seed around so that a whole colony of the next generation plants stand within the same patch. Where the soil is good and enriched with leaf mould foxglove is abundantly happy. It tolerates dappled shade quite well, but in warmer regions it flourishes best in full sunshine, and often benefits from a first winter protection mulch of pine needles applied after the ground has frozen. In areas where the soil is damp, it is advisable to lift the plants in the first autumn (fall), harbouring them in a frame for the winter and replanting them the following spring.

FRAXINELLA

Dictamnus albus (Rutaceae) P

The drug extracted from the root bark is little known today, but it was formerly employed against scrofulous diseases. A tisane from the dried leaves improved digestion and was suggested for nervous complaints and fevers.

In the herb garden fraxinella or burning bush is a dramatic, even flamboyant plant with its plenteous dark leaves and white flowers flaring away from the 30-60 cm- (1-2 ft-) stem during the summer. Good clumps are formed. The main attribute today in the herb garden is the rich balsamic lemon scent of both flowers and leaves. The oil glands are near the surface in the leaves and upper part of the stems, so a light rub releases the scent. But on warm days the volatile oil vaporizes and can be set alight with a match or cigarette lighter. Flames dance about the plant, leaving it unharmed. During dull weather the oil ceases to vaporize and forms a resinous wax around the flowers. It is a native plant of southern and central Europe and Asia Minor.

CULTIVATION Best in full sunshine, when the scent of the volatile oil may be enjoyed. Choose a good fertile, dampish loam for this slow-growing plant and then leave it to its own devices for it resents disturbance. Seed is produced fairly freely, and ought to be sown fresh as it ripens. Sow in boxes or pans, thinning out rather than pricking out, and allow the little plants to develop at their own speed. Once they are bigger, transplant the whole block of compost and seedlings together.

GROUND IVY

Glechoma hederacea (Labiatae) P

A northern European plant that runs across the ground, rooting as it progresses and having wandered over most of Britain, ground ivy crossed the Atlantic and began its onslaught of the American continent from the East. Small pink flowers, minutely spotted with red, rise to about 25 cms (10 ins) at the most, above bountiful prettily marked leaves shaped like those of the ivy.

Gill tea is an old universal remedy for stubborn coughs and to stimulate the kidneys and clarify the blood. In America it used to be taken by painters as a remedy for 'lead colic' and to bathe sore eyes. The name 'gill' comes from the French *guiller*, meaning to ferment beer, the plant having been used to clear beers since Saxon times in Britain. The entire plant possesses a volatile oil bitter in flavour but balsam-like in aroma. Leaves stuffed into the nostrils were considered to relieve a headache; it has also been a component of snuff recipes, for the same reason.

CULTIVATION The trailing square stems root so easily that an 'Irishman's cutting' or piece pulled from an established plant will soon settle in. Specialist seedsmen offer the seed. Ground ivy prefers damper, heavier soils and some sunshine, and can be regarded as a weed suppressor because it tends to become dominant. It will repay careful attention by attracting butterflies to the garden.

Hyssop

Hyssopus officinalis (Labiatae) P

An aromatic shrubby little evergreen with small blue flowers from mid to late summer and tiny leaves, hyssop is a good plant to grow in containers or as an edging. Hailing from southern Europe and cultivated in English gardens since about 1300, it was one of the herbs taken to the New World by the colonists to use in tea and in herbal tobacco, and as an antiseptic.

Pungently aromatic, it used to be used as a strewing herb in medieval days and a pinch or two of the dried herb added to *pot pourri* recipes lend a spicy tone to the mixture. Oil of hyssop was as highly prized in Europe as oil of lavender; it forms an important constituent of Chartreuse.

Hyssop tea made from a few flowers is claimed to relieve catarrh, and for the same reason it was often an ingredient of herbal tobacco. William Turner knew it when he wrote the first book ever to be written in English about English plants (1558) and said, 'The brethe or vapour of Hisop driveth away the Winde that is in the ears, if they be holden over it'. Medicinally, the healing virtues of hyssop are due to a volatile oil which renders it invaluable as a treatment for catarrh, but it also has a reputation for being effective against rheumatism.

CULTIVATION Hyssop is propagated by seed sown in spring, or by cuttings taken in the same season or very early in the summer, and rooted in damp peaty soil in a shaded place. For edging, plant out the rooted cuttings in late summer about 30 cms (1 ft) apart and do not clip for the following summer, but leave the job for 18 months.

Hyssop revels in light, fairly dry, warm soil and does especially well in window-boxes. It is far hardier than is generally realized. Cut growth down in the autumn (fall) to prevent rough winds ripping the plant from its foothold.

JACOB'S LADDER

Polemonium caeruleum (Polemoniaceae) P

Polemonium was the name given by Linnaeus to this genus, commemorating a medicinal plant associated with Polemon of Cappadocia. This species grows sparsely over the whole of the temperate regions of the Northern Hemisphere, although nowhere near as prolifically as some of the other closely related species in America.

In cultivation it is appearing more frequently in representative collections of physic plants although it is no longer used in this way; it is a reasonably common decorative garden perennial. Flowering at midsummer with deep, rich blue flowers and soft, well divided green leaves, it stands up to 40-60 cms (1½-2 ft) high. A hundred years ago it was used as an anti-syphilitic agent and in the treatment of rabies.

False Jacob's Ladder or American Greek valerian is *P. reptans*, indigenous in America from New York to Wisconsin, on damp ground. As a cultivated plant it grows to 30 cms (1 ft) with similar pretty foliage, the blue flower heads nodding. The root of this species is bitter in flavour and is employed as an astringent and against snake bites.

CULTIVATION Choose a moisture-retentive soil in the sunshine to encourage the dainty soft growth of Jacob's Ladder, as this is the plant's main attraction. The flowers are somewhat fleeting, but they occur in succession over three to four weeks. Dead-heading is especially useful. There is a white-flowered form.

Propagation is by division of the creeping rootstock in the dormant season, and once established the plants themselves ensure a succession of generations by seed. It is beloved of cats who roll and rub among the clumps, so sometimes the young plants will need protecting.

JO PYE WEED

Eupatorium purpureum (Compositae) P

Jo Pye was an Indian medicine man in New England who earned fame by curing typhus fever (among other horrors) with this plant. All the *Eupatorium* species are indigenous to the Americas, Africa and Asia; a few are to Europe. Jo Pye weed — or jopi or gravel weed — is a common meadow weed found from Canada to Florida, especially on swampy ground. Its medicinal value lies in its roots, and is particularly useful in treating infirmities relating to the urinary organs. As a strong diuretic it has been employed effectively against gout and rheumatism.

Jo Pye weed was an early introduction into England from America, and is now grown as a hardy herbaceous perennial forming imposing clumps of tall plants, up to 150 cms (5 ft) tall. Particularly useful in the decorative herb garden at the back of the border, hempsweed (as it is sometimes called in England) flowers late in the summer and associates well with the dramatic seed heads of angelica and the blue flowers of borage. The rose-purple fluffy flower heads are held aloft on stately stems decorated by whorls of dark green leaves.

CULTIVATION Provide a dampish soil if possible, or a good soil enriched with compost, leaf mould or some other moisture-retentive material. Divide the clumps in spring or autumn (fall). Seed can also be sown in spring or autumn (fall). In England seed is usually available in 'mixed species' so it will be necessary to grow the plants indoors and select *Eupatorium purpureum* for the herb garden.

LICORICE

Glycyrrhiza glabra (Leguminosae) P

One of the most widely used medicinal plants, licorice has been recorded in cultivation in England since 1562 and was taken to the New World in the following century. Juice from the well-developed root system — which can contain substantial lengths of tap root and stolons — provides the commercial licorice. It has long been used either to mask with its sweetness the unpleasant flavour of other medicines, or provide its own soothing action on troublesome coughs. Even the dried root, stripped of its bitter bark is recommended as a remedy for colds, sore throats and bronchial catarrh. It is the licorice stick of old-fashioned English sweet shops, which children purchased in order to chew the fibrous yellow root, held in the hand like a lollipop. Some heath food shops stock the dried sticks today.

A refreshing 'cure-all' beverage can be made by infusing pieces of the crushed or powdered root in water and adding fennel and lemon and allowing it to stand for 24 hours. The water itself, before the addition of fennel and lemon, makes a good mouthwash, and is especially recommended for a cracked or ulcerated tongue.

Known to the ancient world as *Radix dulcis* (sweet root), licorice does not appear in the wild, although it is thought to be a Middle Eastern plant which arrived in northern Europe via Italy. It is widely cultivated in southern Europe and the southwestern regions of the USSR. In Culpeper's day licorice was a commercially profitable crop, notably in the Pontefract district of Yorkshire in northern England, whence it assumed the name of Pontefract root. Black, hard, glossy 'boot laces' and straps of licorice were manufactured in the area as sweetmeats by concentrating the juice of the root through boiling. Even today, stamped out 'buttons' are sold as Pontefract Cakes in England, and are made in that area from imported licorice. These are thirst quenching and soothing to the digestion and act as a very mild laxative — a use to which licorice has been put for centuries.

A summer flowering plant, it reaches as high as 2 m (6½ ft) with very graceful dark green foliage and spikes of pale violet-blue flowers. Roots are harvested from established plants when three or four years old.

CULTIVATION Pieces of the root, each with a bud, should be planted about 15 cms (6 ins) deep and 1 m (3¼ ft) apart in spring or autumn (fall), or any time during the dormant season when the ground is workable and not frosty. Choose good sandy loam where some moisture is available. Licorice revels in hot summers.

LILY·OF·THE·VALLEY

Convallaria majalis (Liliaceae) P

Country people used to make an infusion of May lily, as it was called, to administer to those suffering from a weak heart. As Gerard pointed out, 'The flower of the Valley Lillie distilled with wine . . . restoreth speech unto those that have the dum palsie and are falne into the Apoplexie'. He claimed also, that it strengthened the memory. Empiricism was well in advance of science for the drug convallamarin constitutes a very powerful cardiac remedy.

Dried flowers reduced to a powder are a powerful sternutatory, claimed to clear the head of nasal mucus, thus relieving ear noises, vertigo and chronic inflammation of the ears.

Richly scented, the flowers of the lily-of-the-valley make an attractive addition to *pot pourri*. Indigenous plants of the lowlands, especially wooded valleys of the temperate zones of the Northern Hemisphere, the far creeping rhizomes form colonies which are quite dense in some situations. Twin, broad, spear-like leaves guard the stiff lower spike of pretty dangling white bells in late spring. *Convallaria montana* of America is generally included with the species *majalis*, and some cultivars are available with superior flowers.

CULTIVATION In the herb garden the plants need to have a moisture-rich soil and some shade to give of their best. The crowns often take some time to become established and may even refuse to strengthen if they are not happy. Plant out corms or divisions of rootstock bearing a growth bud after flowering. (They are best purchased in the summer when the growth buds are plump.) Top dress with leaf mould occasionally when young.

Lily-of-the-valley can be forced in pots for indoor decoration and specially prepared crowns can be purchased for this purpose. Otherwise any good colony can be lifted from the garden in autumn (fall) and the plumpest crown selected for potting up, upright, in a peat compost. Keep the pot in a temperature of about 25 °C (75 °F) to hasten flowering. The plant is unsatisfactory in the warmer and humid zones, but even there it may be grown as a pot plant and kept in the shade.

LUNGWORT

Pulmonaria officinalis (Boraginaceae) P

Lungwort has a fortifying action on the respiratory system, soothing coughs, sore throats and congested tracts, and because of its additional virtue of promoting perspiration, is administered during influenza.

Indigenous to the shaded woodlands of Europe, lungwort has been known in gardens in England for centuries. The flowers resemble those of the cowslip in shade but are pink, mauve or blue according to the stage of development; the pink flowers turn blue after pollination, so intermediate shades can always be found. The vernacular 'cowslip' suggests the American native *Mertensia virginica*, abundant in the mid-west, also known as smooth lungwort and closely allied to the true lungworts. Another colloquial name for *P. officinalis* is spotted bugloss. It has a cucumber-like flavour and was used as a pot herb.

Flowering stems are hairy and grow to a height of 20-30 cms (9-12 ins) and are among the earliest herbs to flower in the spring. The leaves are oval, hairy, rough and spotted.

CULTIVATION Choose a lightly shaded spot with moist, well drained soil. Lungwort displays a slight preference for chalk. Propagation is by spring-sown seed, thinning the seedlings before autumn (fall), or by division of the roots in autumn (fall).

MARSHMALLOW/ENGLISH MALLOW

Althaea officinalis (Malvaceae) P

Great posy-like flowers of the modern hollyhock strung along tall upstanding stalks are a feature of the English cottage garden, but the true officinal plant is altogether daintier and simpler. Often called marshmallow (wymote in America) to distinguish it from its carnival counterpart, the herb is an eastern European native which has emigrated to America where it is an infrequent naturalized plant that grows especially in the vicinity of river estuaries.

It is a velvety perennial plant about 1 m (3¼ ft) tall with smallish pale pink flowers and a boss of reddish anthers in the middle. Thick long roots, tough but pliant, abound in mucilage which is a valuable treatment for coughs and hoarseness, especially in children and the elderly. It is used as an inhalant for sinusitis. A tisane infused from the leaves soothes internal inflammation and makes a gentle eye-bath. Fresh leaves, crushed or pounded to form a poultice, relieve aching muscles, bruised joints and sprains.

The garden hollyhock (*Althaea rosea*), is a tall biennial, attaining a height of 2½ m (8 ft) and has been in English gardens since 1573 when it arrived from China. It has similar constituents but is far milder in effect than the officinal plant; an infusion of the leaves makes a pleasant mouthwash. The leaves of another mallow, the dwarf or blue mallow (*Malva sylvestris*), are used by country people as a poultice to 'draw' boils and carbuncles. The use of both of these plants is superseded by the officinal plant medicinally, but the young leaves of all European mallows can be eaten in salads. The older leaves make a good pot herb and the seeds, known as 'cheeses' (from their shape), are chewed, fresh or dried, as a sweetmeat. A piece of root of the true marshmallow used to be given to teething infants to chew upon for its calming effect. Marshmallow sweets are made from the powdered root only, by soaking in water with sugar until a jelly is formed.

CULTIVATION *Althaea officinalis* is a European native of brackish marshes and therefore appreciates dampish soils. It is propagated by root division in autumn (fall) or early winter, and rarely from seed. Cut back the top growth each autumn (fall) to encourage good lush shoots the following year.

On the other hand, the garden hollyhock is propagated from fresh seed sown in the late summer to flower 18 months later. Alternatively, when it is sown in boxes or pots in the spring, rosettes are formed in the first summer and the growing spike the second. Plant out at the back of the border or against the shelter of a hedge or a wall where the swaying upright spikes can be shown off to advantage.

MILKWORT

Polygala species (Polygalaceae) B

Plants of this genus were named *Polygala* (meaning 'much milk' in Greek) because feeding cows on it is supposed to increase the flow of milk. Numerous species are sparsely distributed on dry banks, heathland and grassy pastures.

The plant cultivated in English herb gardens is *P. vulgaris* and rarely *P. amara*. In American herb gardens it is usually *P. senega*, indigenous to that continent and choosing drier rocky positions than its European counterparts.

The latter specific name commemorates the Seneca Indians who stored the root to treat rattlesnake bites. A Scottish doctor living in Pennsylvania in the 1730s recognized the snake bite symptoms as being very similar to pleurisy and pneumonia, experimented successfully, and introduced *P. senega* into England as an officinal plant in 1739. (Several other species have been cultivated in herb gardens and imported as dried root, indistinguishable from *senega*.)

A really pretty little plant that forms colonies, milkwort is admirably suited to the front of the border in a decorative herb garden. From late spring to mid summer dainty deep blue flowers (white in *P. senega*) dance above the basal foliage rosette. 'Dance' is an accurate description as they resemble tiny elaborately winged insects hovering not more than 5-30 cms (2-12 ins) above the ground-hugging leaves. Roots are small, knotted, often twisted and grey; these are harvested for use in general tonics. The bitter principle relieves chest congestion and acts as a mild laxative. (The supposed influence on lactation in nursing mothers is doubtful.)

CULTIVATION Alkaline soils where the drainage is good suit the milkworts best. The only way to propagate them is from root division of an established plant — unless a source of seed can be traced. (It is not readily available.) A decorative little plant, well worth tracking down to include in the herb garden.

Monkshood/Aconite

Aconitum napellus (Ranunculaceae) P

A highly poisonous plant indigenous to mountainous regions throughout northern temperate zones, monkshood has been cultivated as a healing plant for centuries. According to botanists it is strictly speaking a subspecies of *A. anglicum*. *Aconitum* species provided a poison used for tipping arrows and baiting wolves in medieval Europe, thus earning them the name of 'Wolf's Bane'. Later it became known as monkshood or helmet flower in recognition of its hooded flower. Winthrop's seed order from America in 1631 calls it 'munkhoods'.

A stately garden perennial reaching a height of 60 cms (2 ft) with distinctive deep green firm leaves held fairly horizontal and deeply divided. Deep rich blue flowers bloom in mid summer. Among the garden cultivars worth growing for herb garden decoration are 'Newry Blue' and 'Bressingham Spire'; both reach a height of 90 cms (3ft). The specific name *napellus* means 'little turnip' and describes the shape of the root tuber. Each root lasts only a year; a daughter formed alongside the parent tuber maintains the plant. All parts of the plant are used; the top growth is collected in summer and the root in autumn (fall).

Its toxicity demands that it be prescribed only under medical supervision. Homeopathic preparations are used in the treatment of sciatica and neuralgia as the drug acts upon the central nervous system.

CULTIVATION Sow the seed as soon as it is ripe, but do not expect spectacular results as the plants are slow to establish from seed. Separating a daughter tuber and planting it out in the autumn (fall) will be quicker and probably more successful. Planting can be carried out quite late into the winter, but it must be done before the stem bud bursts into growth — and this happens very early in the spring. Select a well-worked moisture-retentive soil somewhere where there is dappled shade. Monkshood prefers the less humid zones and is winter hardy, but it may need crown protection in low temperature areas.

MOTHERWORT

Leonorus cardiaca (Labiatae) P

Long after this plant became known for its ability to stimulate the heart, recent research has confirmed its pulse regulatory action. Introduced as a cultivated plant from Siberia in 1658, motherwort soon found its way with the colonists to America where it is now a naturalized plant of the country roadsides. New England women prized it for treating all female complaints and knew of its value as a fertility drug, a regulator of menstruation and effective in relieving stomach cramps. Culpeper says, rather quaintly, 'Besides it makes Women joyful Mothers of children and settles their wombs as they should be, therefore we call it Motherwort. . . . It is held to be of so much Use for the Trembling of the Heart, and Faintings and Swoonings, from whence it took the name Cardiaca'.

Horizontally-growing underground stems support the stiff square reddish flower stalks 60-100 cms (2-3½ ft) tall which are punctuated by pairs of large stiff leaves. Around the stem are whorls of many tiny pink flowers, spotted red. The whole plant gives off an unpleasant smell.

CULTIVATION Once established motherwort will survive the hardest of winters in Europe and all but the central climatic zones of America. Good upstanding clumps will form in a year or two in any good garden soil. By cutting away a horizontally-creeping stem with growth buds and planting it elsewhere in autumn (fall) new clumps can be formed.

OPIUM POPPY

Papaver somniferum (Papaveraceae) A

Opium is a dangerous and addictive poison but it remains unsurpassed as a sedative administered for the relief of pain — a consequence of its two important alkaloids, morphine and codeine. Opium was a medicine known to the Greeks and Romans and the Egyptians before them, and the cultivation of the poppy spread to China more than 1,000 years ago.

The flowers vary considerably in appearance; they are sometimes double, sometimes single with flimsy mauve petals — occasionally white or pink. When the buds open the petals are like crumpled tissue paper balls, which very quickly unfold; this is a feature of the plant. Handsome in its stance, the plant attains perhaps 1 m (3¼ ft) in height, the blue-green-grey leaves sitting directly on the stem and held away from it, with jagged wavy margins.

Once the petals fall the seed head matures into the familiar smooth brown 'poppy head' with its lid of radiating ribs and little holes round the top through which the seeds escape. Opium is a form of latex which oozes out of the unripe seed heads when they are slit. Unripe poppy heads used to be infused to bathe swollen and sprained joints, and a fermentation made with hot barley meal as a binding agent was used in similar instances to relieve pain.

There are many types of poppy seed; the blue-grey tiny rounded ones are used in Europe and America to decorate and flavour bread and confectionery, and the smaller creamy ones are habitually used in India to thicken curries. Poppy seed oil, although a culinary oil (olivette), is commonly prepared for the industrial market and in the mixing of paints.

A native of the Middle East and the Mediterranean countries, the mauve flowers are a roadside feature of some southern counties of England. Poppies were taken as seed to America and appear in the 1631 order from John Winthrop Jr as 'popey seed'.

CULTIVATION Propagate from seed sown afresh each spring, although once introduced into the herb garden the plants will seed themselves. Lovers of sunshine, light warm soils and tolerant of chalk, the opium poppy ought to be in every representative collection of medicinal herbs.

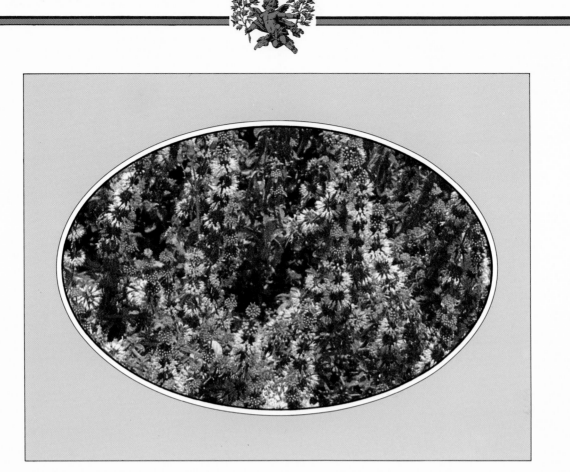

PENNYROYAL

Mentha pulegium (Labiatae) P

Like all other mints pennyroyal is highly aromatic, but its flavour is more acid and less refined than that of spearmint or peppermint. Two kinds are cultivated; one is a trailing plant no more than 10 cms (4 ins) high with a prostrate habit which roots as it progresses over the ground to gain a foothold. The other is upright in stance — about 25 cms (10 ins) — and is the best form to cultivate and is easier to harvest. Both bear small oval leaves in pairs with tiny lilac flowers in whorls abut the stems and bloom in high summer. Pennyroyal was known to the Romans as an insect deterrent and was used to expel fleas from clothes and palliasses.

Pennyroyal is a denizen of ditches in Europe and parts of Asia and is considered to be one of the plants that the Pilgrim Fathers took from England to the New World (where it became known as organie). It is a valuable treatment for purifying blood, headaches, hoarseness, nausea and more importantly against 'mother fits' (a Saxon word for hysterics).

Pennyroyal is perhaps best known as a purifier of water. Years ago it was carried on long sea voyages to purify the casks of drinking water. Gerard knew it for this purpose and Culpeper said, 'Put into unwholesome waters . . . that men must drink, it makes them the less hurtful'. He also advised its use 'to expel the dead child and afterbirth'. Externally, it soothed bruises, healed 'green wounds' and cleared spots and blemishes, ulcers and 'the marks of Bruises and Blows'.

CULTIVATION A good ground cover herb, pennyroyal enjoys a damp position where there is a good deal of shade. Plant it among paving stones where its roots can run about in the cool soil. Both the creeping and the upright sort will enhance a garden patio corner or a herb garden pathway. It should be lifted and moved indoors in areas where the temperature falls below − 15°C (5°F).

POKEWEED

Phytolacca americana (Syn. *P. decandra*) (Phytolaccaceae) P

Pokeweed, pokeberry, pokeroot, stoke — call it what you will — is indigenous to the warm temperate zones of America. A plant of roadside thickets and waste land, it was introduced into cultivation in England from Florida in 1768, when it was named American poke. It has a reputation as a remedy for internal cancers — hence its earlier name of cancer root.

A remarkable feature of the plant is that the young shoots may be eaten as asparagus, but as they mature the root which provides the active principle becomes increasingly poisonous. A shrubby plant whose erect stems are tubular, up to 1.5-2 m (5-6 ft) tall, branching towards the top, it is frequently suffused with red (especially as the season advances). In England the plant is virtually a clump-forming herbaceous perennial.

Egg-shaped light green leaves are surmounted by a firm spike of greenish white flowers in late summer. Deep damson purple berries follow, ripening in autumn (fall) to provide a rich dye.

Its purgative narcotic properties are effective in relieving stubborn headaches and may be employed internally in cases of rheumatism and arthritis, and externally in the control of some skin conditions.

Phytolacca clavigera, a similar plant with spikes of pale pink flowers followed by maroon berries, is cultivated in some herb gardens and provides a powerful emetic and narcotic which must not be used except under reputable medical supervision.

CULTIVATION Plant in spring or autumn (fall) in good moisture-retentive soil in a spot sheltered from wind, in either sun or partial shade. Propagation is by division in spring or by seed sown when ripe in late summer.

Rue

Ruta graveolens (Rutaceae) P

This well-known member of the herb border, highly regarded in old country medicine all over Europe, is a native of the dusty soils of the Mediterranean regions. The Romans reputedly introduced it into Britain first, although it was probably reintroduced in the Middle Ages. It went to the New World with the European settlers, where it is now naturalized in some southern states on low quality soils. Herb of Grace, was one of its old names, and Parkinson explained it thus: 'The many good properties whereunto Rue serveth hath I think in former times caused the English name of Herbe of Grace to be given unto it'. Holy water was sprinkled as a preliminary to the celebration of High Mass in the medieval Church from switches made of rue twigs. Its reputation for repelling infection and poison made it customary for sprigs of rue to be placed near the judge before prisoners were brought from the pestilence-ridden gaols.

Just why it was held in such high esteem is difficult to assess; today its bitter flavour — dispersed by pulverizing or chopping — can be added, with discretion, to egg, fish or cream cheese dishes. In European wine-growing areas rue leaves are added to brandy to make a liqueur. The rather sombre little bushes were also thought to form an unfailing defence against witches and to grant a sixth sense. Renaissance painters in Europe are reputed to have consumed large quantities of rue tea to restore failing eyesight.

Rue is a dainty bushy plant 45-90 cms (1½-3 ft) in height with blue-green ferny leaves and greenish yellow spoon-shaped flowers during the summer. The entire plant emits a somewhat harsh aroma and has an equally harsh taste as a result of the volatile oil contained in the glands which are distributed over the whole plant. Medicinally rue is toxic in high doses and should be used with prudence, especially during pregnancy, as it has an ancient reputation for starting delayed periods. It is also used to treat bites and stings externally and, as a cold compress applied to the temples, it is said to relieve nervous headaches.

CULTIVATION Raised from seed sown in spring and thinned out to about 50 cms (1½ ft) apart, rue can make a good herb garden hedge and its evergreen nature lends itself to this use. Cuttings taken in summer will strike quite easily. Rue revels in a well drained soil and loves a sunny sheltered site. It benefits from being cut back in the spring to encourage new fresh growth.

SELF HEAL

Prunella vulgaris (Labiatae) P

A native of the temperate regions of the Northern Hemisphere from Asia to Europe, and although probably naturalized in North America, self heal is sufficiently common to be called 'heart of the earth'. It is an inhabitant of waste land, pasture and woodland verges and it is regarded as a persistent weed in many English gardens.

Self heal was often combined with bugle (*Ajuga reptans*) to form an astringent which staunched the bleeding of open wounds. A tisane made from the whole herb, sweetened with honey, is considered to be soothing for sore throats or for use as a gargle or mouthwash to alleviate ulcers of the tongue.

It varies in height according to the conditions in which it grows, and ranges from a ground-hugging spreading weed to a boldly upstanding plant 45 cms (1½ ft) tall. Mauve flowers and bracts together form a quite distinctive terminal flower head which is barrel-shaped. The leaves are dark green and diamond-shaped.

CULTIVATION Self heal appears unheralded in many gardens, but there is a pretty pink flowered form available from some herb nurseries and specialist seedsmen. Sow seed at any time from spring to autumn (fall); try to avoid waterlogged sites.

SOLOMON'S SEAL

Polygonatum multiflorum (Liliaceae) P

The hybrid *P. multiflorum × odoratum* is probably the most common representative of the genus in gardens, although *multiflorum* is the true officinal plant and is a native of Europe.

Solomon's seal was traditionally cultivated for its creeping rootstock which provided a tonic and astringent; the powdered root was applied to bruises and tumorous haemorrhoids to relieve pain. As an application for black eyes it was known to the battered wives of the fifteenth and sixteenth centuries, for Gerard wrote, 'The roots of Solomon's seal, stamped while fresh and greene and applied taketh away in one night or two at the most, any bruise blacke or blew spots gotten by fals or womens' wilfulness in stimbling upin their hastie husband's fists, or such like'. Gerard thought that for the knitting of broken bones 'there is not another herb to be found comparable to it'.

The plant has for centuries been employed as a cosmetic to clear freckles and as a skin tonic. In Turkey the young shoots, which are folded spikes of green, are harvested and cooked with asparagus.

Solomon's seal is a truly memorable plant. It has a fabulous aura with its pale green stems stretching up to a height of 60 cms (2 ft) arching over gracefully at the top. Large oval leaves alternate along the top half like wings above the dangling waxy white bell flowers.

CULTIVATION Given a well-worked, light and moisture-retentive soil where there is a little shade, Solomon's seal will soon establish sizeable colonies. An occasional top dressing of leaf mould is beneficial. The plants are best divided just after the stalks die down in the autumn (fall), although in dampish weather transplanting and division can be undertaken at any time of the year. Seed, when available, should be sown as soon as it is ripe in the late summer or early autumn (fall).

Thorn Apple

Datura stramonium (Solanaceae) A

Not surprisingly, thorn apple is known in America as Jimson or Jamestown weed, since it was around the Jamestown settlement that it first became colonized. The people responsible for taking thorn apple to America were either Raleigh's 'colonists' or a group of marauding Spaniards. As a native of temperate regions it must have established itself immediately, for it became a familiar weed of docks, barn yards and waste land (showing a marked predilection for rank soils which reflected its own rank smell). In Britain thorn apple is extremely rare and is usually only found on waste land — it can hardly be considered to be naturalized.

A large coarse herb, thorn apple has (when fully grown) long and large strongly veined leaves with a wavy toothed margin. Plants are cultivated for their leaves, which are poisonous until dried, and, unlike most herbs, the plants are at their richest when in full flower. The flowers are white, long, tubular and have deep leaf axils; they are in bloom for a long period during the summer. Thorn apple is the name given to the seed capsules; each one resembles a large green gooseberry covered with numerous spines. The black seeds are highly poisonous — thus the American name Devil's apple. A tincture of the seeds is still prescribed occasionally today in the treatment of asthma. In general, thorn apple, like its close relative belladonna, has a sedative action, dilating the pupils of the eyes.

CULTIVATION Very poor quality soil will support thorn apple, but when grown in good soil replenished with compost or manure, really good specimens can be grown to provide a curious plant that attracts attention. Sow the seed in spring *in situ* or in pots, planting out the little plants later into prepared beds as for marrows. In America it thrives in all but the coldest zones with temperatures lower than $-7\,°C\,(20\,°F)$, provided that it is on a really dusty soil.

VALERIAN

Valeriana officinalis (Valerianaceae) P

Valerian is a native of the temperate zones of Europe and Asia, and is pretty indifferent to the soil and situation it selects. It is often found in dampish valleys and on dry stony elevated pastures. A plant for the back of the herb border, the flower stems reach a height of 1.5 m (5 ft) with pretty dark ferny leaves at the base and clustered heads of pink (and occasionally white) flowers in the summer. Roots are lifted in the second and third year in the autumn and are thick and clustered. After washing they need to be 'combed' before drying in the shade.

Valerian was formerly cultivated for its root, and was introduced into America in the eighteenth century. It was cultivated extensively in eastern Europe, the Netherlands and in America in New Hampshire, Vermont and New York. When grown for its root, the flowering stems are removed to encourage development of the rhizome. The ancient name was phu (or phew); a name that reflected the bad-smelling newly lifted root. It is reputed to be the charm the Pied Piper of Hamelin used to lead the rats away.

Valerian is administered as a painkiller and nervine, and is especially useful in calming nervous disorders and in treating insomnia.

CULTIVATION Propagation is by division of roots or stolons in autumn (fall) or spring. In the herb garden, plant it in a good moisture-retentive soil to obtain lush decorative plants. In America, where seed sets readily, seed can be sown in spring by just pressing it into the ground. Most gardeners buy their first plant, then depend upon the seed for a continued crop.

WHITE HOREHOUND/COMMON HOREHOUND

Marrubium vulgare (Labiatae) P

The silky hairs that adorn this plant give it a frosty, almost dusty appearance which is emphasized by whorls of tiny white flowers in midsummer. Square-stemmed and fibrously tough, especially at the base, it grows to a height of 60 cms (2 ft) and has wrinkled leaves blistered and hairy. Harvested just as the plants come into flower when the essential oil is richest, the dry leaves have been utilized as a country remedy for centuries. The Romans used it as an insecticide. A candy made with sugar was a household remedy for our grandmothers, and the bitter tisane served to revive reluctant appetites. The same preparation has been used externally as an application to wounds and bruises as an antiseptic.

Gerard claimed that it 'doth wonderfully and above credit ease such as have been long sicke of any consumption of the lungs, as hathe beene often proved by learned physitions of our London College'.

In America white hyssop is considered to be naturalized, although there seems to be no record of its introduction from Europe where it is a none too frequent weed associated with dwellings and obsolete rubbish tips.

CULTIVATION Choose a loose dry soil in a fully sunlit spot for horehound in the herb garden. Propagate by root division during the dormant season at any time that the soil is open and not frosted, although in some gardens it is known to self-seed.

WITCH HAZEL

Hamamelis virginiana (Hamamelidiaceae) P

The witch hazel from the woodlands of eastern America has much in common in appearance with the European hazel. Various explanations are proffered as to why the settlers called this shrub witch hazel. Perhaps the most acceptable is that they used the twigs for water divining in much the same manner in which they had used hazel at home — commonly called 'witching a well'. But they soon learned of its invaluable quality as an astringent, its ability to check bleeding, and as a treatment for bruises and bumps. The American Indians had used the bark to make an infusion to apply to sore eyes. Today, witch hazel remains a household remedy, as an extract that can be bought from pharmacies for use as a skin tonic and as an ointment to soothe sprains and bruises.

However, unlike those of the European hazel the seeds of the American plant are ejected with enough force to bombard passers-by, and this puckish quirk has gained it the name of snapping hazelnut. Witch hazel is a shrub which grows to a height of 3-3.6 m (10-12 ft). The leaves are more heavily veined than those of the European hazel, and once they have fallen in autumn the flowers appear on the bare wood within a month. These flowers are lovely little fluffy clusters of yellow which on inspection turn out to be bundles of tiny strap-shaped petals with a very faint scent. Seed ripens the following summer, the nuts containing two black seeds, oily and edible. Seed does not set in England.

Both leaves and bark have the astringent property for which the plant is renowned. In England the old nineteenth century Pond's Extract depended upon witch hazel for its effectiveness as a household panacea used in cases of burns and bruises.

CULTIVATION A shrub that makes a very welcome addition to the herb garden in areas free from early frosts, where it can be enjoyed unspoilt. However, the attractive foliage and curious strap-shaped petals will withstand the severest autumn (fall) quite well. Propagation is by cuttings taken in spring.

YARROW

Achillea millefolium (Cruciferae) P

Yarrow, or sneezewort (as it is sometimes known), is a common road and woodside plant in both Europe and America which is so abundant that it is scarcely noticed. For centuries it was used to staunch wounds and control excessive bleeding. European gypsies had their own name for it — carpenter's herb — always at hand for when a workman's tool slipped. And yet at the same time it was employed to cause nose-bleeding for the relief of headaches. This was effected by stuffing the leaves up the nostrils which resulted in violent sneezing, bringing on a nosebleed. Its widespread use as a vulnerary is testified to by its string of old names: knight's milfoil, herbe militaris, bloodwort and staunchweed.

The stem is tough and difficult to break, not completely upstanding — only 50 cms (1½ ft) tall and adorned with plenteous dark green feathery leaves. The entire plant is more or less hairy and dusty in appearance. Chalk white flowers with black middles bloom in flattish heads during the summer and early autumn.

Early in the summer the leaves may be added chopped, with restraint, to salads before the advancing season renders them too peppery. When dried they constitute a good tisane which may be used as a circulation enlivener and promoter of perspiration to be administered in the early stages of a fever, cold or bout of childhood measles.

Culpeper claimed that this infusion cured cramp, and modern herbalism uses it externally as a skin cleanser, especially for oily skins. Chew fresh leaves to relieve toothache.

CULTIVATION Propagate from seed or root division. Specialist seedsmen offer seed for spring sowing and seedlings may be dotted about the herb border as yarrow has a reputation for improving the condition of plants in its vicinity. From seed the plants may prove slow to establish, taking a year or two to develop (even in dry warm regions) as the plants are drought-tolerant.

YELLOW GENTIAN

Gentiana lutea (Gentianaceae) P

The yellow gentian, or drug gentian as it is known in America, is a denizen of the alpine meadows of Europe. It was the first of its genus to arrive in Britain and Gerard grew it in his garden. Once seen it is never forgotten for it is a statuesque plant holding itself poker straight to a height of 90-150 cms (3-5 ft). The leaves, in pairs, clasp the stem to form cups at intervals which are filled with golden yellow starry flowers.

It is a very long-lived perennial which first forms a rosette of leaves before flowering. The roots plunge 1 m (3¼ ft) into the earth and these are harvested to render gentian bitters. Sometimes they are stored and fermented before distillation — as required in the *British Pharmacopoeia*, when the root assumes a yellowish brown colour. Infusions and tinctures are used to fortify medicine as appetite stimulants or in the preparation of gentian bitters. In veterinary medicine it provides an appetiser. The bruised fresh leaves make a soothing antiseptic dressing for wounds and inflammation.

CULTIVATION Yellow gentian can be grown from seed, but takes many years to flower — a single plant can survive a couple of generations. Root cuttings are thus the more usual method of propagation, and they need to be planted out once sprouted into deep, rich soil where the gigantic root can develop and forage. It is not suitable for **growing in places that have warm winters.**

SWEET SCENTED HERBS

Pot Pourri

UTHORS of the early herbals expressed a widespread belief in the power of flower and leaf scents to alleviate all manner of ills of the flesh and spirit, and as unfailing protection against infections. Scented conceits such as *pot pourri* probably originated in England in Tudor times. Wands of aromatic plants were strewn on floors to absorb rubbish, alleviate strong smells and discourage vermin; it was merely a refinement to harbour together the sweet-smelling flowers and leaves of summer in jars or pouncet boxes (small containers with a perforated lid) or even open bowls.

Pot pourri translated literally from the French means 'rotten pot' because in the early days of *pot pourri* the mixtures were kept moist and the flowers virtually pickled. Brandy or some other spirit provided and maintained the moisture. Such a richly aromatic preserve was usually kept in closed containers, opened only infrequently when a room was to be perfumed.

Dry *pot pourri* is more popular today and is far less arduous to prepare, less rich in aroma and, naturally, not so long lasting. Essentially, *pot pourri* is a homogeneous mixture of dried aromatic leaves, scented flower petals with spices and perhaps a fragrant oil and some fixative to retain the scent. A captive mixture can be controlled to suit individual preference — herby, flowery, spicy or aromatic.

Scented powders in sachets, dried aromatic leaves or little bunches of scented plants were hung in cupboards or laid among clothes in chests to keep them fresh. Aromatic sprigs were burned on fires or in special censers, usually of bronze or copper, to set scented smoke pervading the room.

When the European colonists arrived in America they soon found that the berries of the wax myrtle, sweet gale or bayberry provided a fragrant wax which could be collected and burned to give a delicious aroma. Scented candles and wood chips are traditionally associated with religion, but the practice of scenting houses in this way goes back to classical times.

OPPOSITE *Chamomile paths lead up to the central sundial in the scented garden at Hatfield House.*

ALECOST

Chrysanthemum balsamita Syn. *Balsamita major* (Compositae) P

Alecost or costmary came from the Middle East and was known to the ancient world; the Romans probably brought it first to Britain. It was taken to America by the seventeenth-century colonists and now grows as a garden escape along roadsides in eastern and mid-western states.

The leaves are green, ovate and have a light bloom. Small, yellow button-like flowers appear in July and August. The plant reaches some 60-90 cms (2-3 ft) in height. In America it goes by the name of Bible leaf because early settlers used the beautiful leaf as a Bible marker, and the slightly balsam-mint aroma sweetened the book. Sweet washing water was also made from this plant.

A trace chopped into a salad adds a subtle flavour, slightly spicy, and one that also goes well with game, poultry, veal and cold meats. Formerly employed in the making of beer or ale and sometimes added to sage tea, alecost was bestowed with numerous healing virtues by the Tudor herbalists in England.

Alecost leaves dry well and retain their sweet aroma so they may be incorporated in *pot pourri*. Dried leaves can be used with lavender to make nosegay sachets.

CULTIVATION If possible select a sunny position (although alecost grows in most positions). Sow seed in spring if it is available. Where alecost does not set seed, it can be obtained from specialist seedsmen. Otherwise, take a creeping rooted portion of the established plant to plant out independently in spring.

A pestle and mortar are particularly useful for breaking up and mixing fresh herbs for culinary purposes (OPPOSITE BELOW). *This* pot pourri *consists largely of whole parts of herbs which must be mixed by hand* (OPPOSITE ABOVE).

BERGAMOT

Monarda didyma (Labiatae) P

A handsome plant indigenous to South America and the eastern parts of America from New York to West Virginia, bergamot is an inhabitant of swampy stream borders in hilly areas. It was introduced into Britain around 1745 and is now well established as a decorative garden perennial, and is the parent of many cultivars.

The plant is quick to grow and forms clumps with numerous stolons. The flower stems grow to a height of 50-90 cms (1½-3 ft) and flower for many weeks from mid summer onwards. The entire plant is impregnated with a delightful fragrance even when the top growth has died down, and the roots remain sweetly aromatic with a suggestion of orange. This is why it has gained its name of bergamot, reminiscent of bergamot orange. The aromatic leaves dry well and retain their aroma so they may be included in *pot pourri*.

A tisane made from the leaves used to be drunk by the Oswego Indians — hence the country name Oswego tea. This infusion is recommended as a digestive and is helpful in treating cases of irregular and painful menstruation.

The flowers are a flamboyant red and are born in heads with red bracts between each floret, the whole resembling a sparkler firework. Reliable cultivars are available with pink, mauve and white flowers, all of which retain the aromatic attributes which make them extremely useful in the decorative herb garden — they all attract bees! The flowers make a decorative addition to fruit cups, but should be floated in water first to wash out the earwigs that love to hide in the little tubular florets.

The genus *Monarda* commemorates Nicholas Monardes, a doctor from Seville, who in 1569 wrote his reputable account of the economic plants, including medicinal, that he found in the New World. *Monarda fistulosa*, wild bergamot, was the first of the genus to reach England in 1637.

CULTIVATION Bergamot is best suited to moist soil, or any good garden soil to which moisture-retentive material has been added, and it loves to sunbathe. It is quite adaptable to a shaded position provided its feet remain damp. Chalky soils do not suit it at all well and it dislikes humid winters because its annual growth cycle is hindered.

A piece pulled from the outer edges of an established clump in spring will soon establish itself, and cuttings may be taken at the same time. The clumps form a mat-like growth and tend to become bare in the middle, so they need to be broken up and divided every three or four years.

CALAMINTHA

Calamintha nepetoides (Labiatae) P

The calamintha often found in herb gardens is *C. nepetoides*, although the true herb is *C. ascendens* — a European native, formerly the officinal plant, and at that time called *C. officinalis*. Both plants seem to have been used in the past without distinction.

    A small, erect, bushy little plant 30-60 cms (1-2 ft) in height, calamintha has tiny, whitish mauve flowers in summer. Grown for its aromatic foliage reminiscent of the scent of thyme with pennyroyal overtones, it was mainly employed to relieve flatulence. The volatile oil, rather minty in flavour, enhances a tisane brewed from the dried leaves and which Gerard considered to take away 'sorrowfulness which cometh with melancholie, and maketh a man merrie and glad'. Culpeper described it as having a fierce and quick scent and called it mountain mint and, as usual, recommended its use for a wide variety of complaints ranging from shortness of breath, cramp, liver and spleen trouble, combined with salt to clear worms and as a contraceptive.

CULTIVATION Division of plants in spring, cuttings in spring and seed are all ways to start this little old-fashioned plant in the herb garden. Choose a dryish alkaline soil for the best results.

FLORENTINE IRIS

Iris florentina (Iridaceae) P

Stately irises have represented power and majesty since ancient times and this Macedonian plant was widely cultivated in Italy. The poet Dante mentions that the ancient arms of the city of Florence bore a white iris on a red shield; the iris was the classic flower of a floral area — hence Florence.

The white flowers usually have a lavender trim on the petals and a good fan of typical iris leaves. The flower stems grow to about 60 cms (2 ft) high, but in warm regions reach 1.5 m (5 ft). The rhizome provides the orris root used in perfumery and medicine, though no longer in the vast quantities seen in the eighteenth and nineteenth centuries when Italy and France exported orris all over the world. .

Gerard knew the Florentine iris as a garden plant; it was not cultivated commercially in England, and it was not the plant taken from Europe to America by the settlers; that was *I. pseudacorus*.

Orris root was used in the past in the preparation of the sweet powders used for storing linen and in chests and cupboards. When first harvested the root maintains its earthy smell, but on drying develops a violet-like aroma — perhaps not its strongest until about two years after lifting. The amateur herbalist can peel and slice, or chop or powder the dried root successfully. The little pieces are valuable when added to *pot pourri* as they act as a fixative, absorbing and at the same time pervading the mixed sweet-scented ingredients.

CULTIVATION As with most irises the Florentine iris takes a while to establish itself. The knobbly rhizomes do not begin to develop until the third year after planting. Select a sunny well-drained site where the colony can be left alone to look after itself for a while. Plant the rhizomes in mid to late summer , after the flowering period, and keep the rhizome horizontal to the soil surface.

Iris

Iris pseudacorus (Iridaceae) P

Two or three native European irises have been used in medicine, the best known, the yellow flag iris, is British and was the variety taken to America by the early settlers. In America this plant is called blue flag, the flowers being violet blue and variegated with yellow, and the flower stems attaining 60-90 cms (2-3 ft) in height. Iris has long been cultivated in America for its roots which are used to treat bumps and bruises, and as iridin (or irisin) for its action on the liver and bowels.

The true yellow flag bears small, elegant, golden yellow flowers in summer, and is a fairly common plant of waterway borders and marshy ground in Britain. Flowering stems and sword-like leaves reach a height of 60-150 cms (2-5 ft) and the plants can form extensive colonies. Universally known as *fleur de luce* or *fleur de lys* it was the heraldic emblem of the kings of France and legends abound on that score. The specific name *pseudacorus* acknowledges its resemblance when not in flower to the sweet sedge or sweet flag, *Acorus calamus*. However, the foliage and roots of iris are odourless whereas sweet sedge is aromatic.

The powdered root is an ingredient of snuff, and when sliced can provide a cure for toothache. Culpeper extolled its use, when distilled, as a remedy for weak and tired eyes and maintained that an ointment made from the flowers was good for treating ulcers or even syphilitic sores. The flowers produce a good yellow dye and the roots, with the addition of an iron mordant, produce a black dye.

CULTIVATION Yellow flag can only be grown successfully as a water plant. In the decorative herb garden it needs a boggy area where it can accompany water mints, sweet sedge, watercress, bogbean or brooklime. Settle the rhizomes into the borders of a muddy pool and, if necessary, tie some rhizomes together in a string or wire bag which can be weighted to prevent the clumps from floating away.

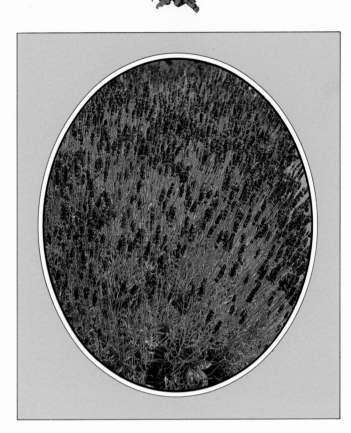

LAVENDER

Lavandula species (Labiatae) P

The best oil of lavender is obtained from *L. angustifolia*, which botanists recently seem to have included under the blanket name of *L. spica*. Gerard called it 'spike' which should settle the question because the old herbalists knew that spike lavender was the best one to grow. (Alternative names — and authorities differ — are *L. vera* and *L. officinalis*.)

For centuries the effectiveness of its clean sharp scent has been used to alleviate 'a light migram' as Gerard said, or for the falling sickness or giddiness of the brain according to Culpeper. Long before the world of manufactured deodorants and bath salts the Romans used lavender in their bath water; the name derives from the Latin *lavare*, to wash.

Lavender is one of the most popular plants in today's herb gardens and is particularly useful in borders to pathways, edges, internal hedges and on top of dry walls. Furthermore, it can be cultivated in large containers. Small grey abundant leaves, evergreen in Europe and England, form a rounded bush 90-180 cms (3-6 ft) high, and sometimes more in spread, which is punctuated with stiff-stemmed lavender-blue flower heads. The whole plant resembles a large pincushion. In America lavender is not regarded as a hardy evergreen because of the low winter temperatures, but if grown in containers in yards and tucked up for the winter its summer fragrance can be enjoyed.

Lavender is not really considered to be a culinary herb, but the odd leaf may be added to rich game stews. The flowers can be crystallized to decorate desserts and confectionery. Its most enduring quality is its perfume, and it is a marvellous *pot pourri* ingredient.

CULTIVATION Propagate from cuttings of strong new growth in summer or autumn (fall), and once rooted plant them out in a well drained rather poor soil. The bushes tend to look after themselves and respond to an annual haircut in autumn after flowering or in early spring. Bushes tend to straggle as they mature and it is often necessary to cut back severely in autumn (fall) to generate a strong growth the following spring. It is wise to maintain a supply of young plants.

ROSE

Rosa gallica officinalis (Rosaceae) P

Numerous mythological and romantic associations have surrounded the rose through the centuries and belief in its unfailing powers led to its uses in medicine and sweet-smelling confections.

Rosa gallica officinalis is the apothecary's rose, known somewhat misleadingly in England as the damask rose because it was brought back to Europe by the crusaders from Damascus. In America is is called the French rose, or rose of Provins. Because the dried petals hold their fragrance it has been widely used in the manufacture of various perfumes — especially in the area of the town of Provins, south of Paris, during the sixteenth, seventeenth and eighteenth centuries.

The plant is a bush some 60-120 cms (2-4 ft) in height, thick and spreading, and a good plant for an informal hedge around the herb garden. The leaves are a good dark green, composed of five leaflets, and the stiff bristly stems are virtually thornless. The petals are bright red with a golden cluster of anthers at the open centre.

In the past, rose honey, lozenges, rose scented snuff and rose scented candles, rose scented wine, rose vinegar and rose sauce were all widely available. Fresh or dried petals can be scattered on salads and desserts or floated in drinks and the hips can be gently boiled until soft, strained, and the liquid used as a tisane.

In perfumery, because the petals retain so strong a scent on drying, they were invaluable for sweet waters and sweet bags and they are the predominant ingredient of *pot pourri*.

CULTIVATION Roses love the sunshine and need some moisture at the roots. Basic cultivation is the same for all roses, although the complicated pruning routine associated with modern roses does not have to be followed for the apothecary's rose. Merely remove dead and old branches; if too much pruning is undertaken the energy of the plant will be directed into making growth rather than producing flowers.

In America this rose will thrive in all but the very northerly regions, and likes some winter cold in order to have its winter rest. Many gardeners consider its cultivation impractical, and it is certainly not for the southern and western seaboard states. (There the Cherokee rose, *R. laevigata* is a carefree grower.)

Choose good garden loam, and prepare the soil well before planting in the autumn (fall) or spring. It is advisable to buy small plants as propagation from cuttings can be a rather slow process. In areas where the winter temperature falls below − 12°C (10°F) bushes planted in autumn (fall) should be covered during their first winter with a protective mulch (which can be removed the following spring).

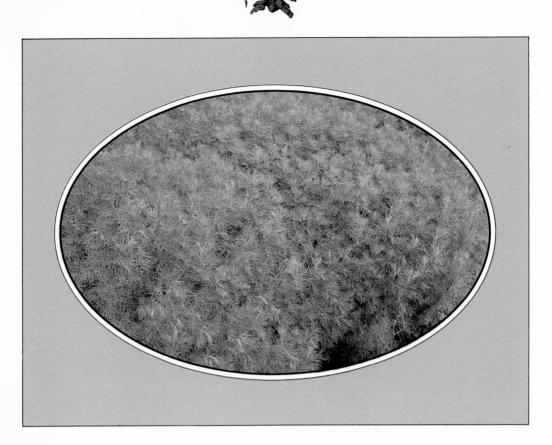

SOUTHERNWOOD

Artemisia abrotanum (Compositae) P

Lad's love, or southernwood, is a delightful aromatic herb. The soft green feathery foliage is silky to touch and invites the hand to brush it in passing to release the sweet camphor aroma. The individual leaves are so finely indented as to appear almost lace-like, so it is the whole sprays of foliage that are dried to add to *pot pourri* and scent sachets. Sprays put in cupboards among clothes make an effective moth repellent — hence its old name of *garde robe*. Culpeper recommended an ointment of southernwood to kill head lice. He also, rather quaintly, suggested its use with boiled breadcrumbs as an application for sore eyes.

At home in the Mediterranean countries, southernwood was known in English gardens in Tudor times.

CULTIVATION Southernwood appreciates a well drained soil enriched with some leaf mould or compost, and needs to be protected from strong winds. Take cuttings of the new growth in early summer, or hard wood cuttings with a heel in autumn (fall). Leave all the growth on through the winter in spite of its bedraggled appearance (which has earned it the colloquial name of old man) as this growth will protect the woody stems from the effect of cold winds. Cut back in early spring to produce lush fresh growth. Only hardy in more temperate regions.

WORMWOOD

Artemisia absinthium (Compositae) P

A native of Europe including Britain, wormwood is one if the most magical plants of the herb garden. It has been introduced into America as a cultivated plant and is now naturalized in places.

Wormwood is primarily a flavouring for liqueurs and aperitifs — such as absinth and vermouth — because it has a unique fragrance. The pale green deeply cut leaves (which are silvery when young) provide a highly decorative foil in the herb garden. It is a little woody-based bush which glistens in the dew and rain. Rounded bushes grow up to 90-120 cms (3-4 ft) tall and produce green-yellow flowers in summer. The leaves are sweetest in aroma when gathered early in the summer.

In spacious herb gardens a splendid effect can be achieved by grouping several bushes together. It can be grown in containers and, where winter cold poses problems, taken into shelter during the winter. Add youngish leaves to *pot pourri* and herb sachets, and scatter dried sprigs in drawers and cupboards to keep the air fresh. The essential oil of wormwood is produced from this plant in both France and America.

CULTIVATION Propagate from summer cuttings or from seed sown as soon as it is ripe, and protect through the winter. Both dappled shade or full sunshine are suitable for wormwood, but bushes do appreciate some shelter from strong winds.

DIRECTORY

OF PLANT

NAMES

ENGLISH	AMERICAN	BOTANICAL NAME
Aaron's rod	garden mullein	*Verbascum nigrum*
acorus sweet flag myrtle grass myrtle sedge	sweet flag calamus root flag root	*Acorus calamus*
agrimony church steeples liverwort	tall agrimony agrimony stickweed	*Agrimonia eupatoria*
alecost costmary	Bible leaf alecost costmary mint geranium	*Chrysanthemum balsamita* *Tanacetum balsamita*
alexanders alexandrian parsley black lovage	(not known in N. America)	*Smyrnium olusatrum*
alkanet	alkanet	*Pentaglottis sempervirens*
allspice Californian allspice	Carolina allspice Californian allspice	*Calycanthus floridus* *C. occidentalis*
American burnet	American great burnet	*Sanguisorba canadensis*
American mandrake	May apple hog apple	*Podophyllum peltatum*
American poke	**pokeweed** pokeberry poke pokeroot	*Phytolacca americana*
American sarsaparilla	wild sarsaparilla false sarsaparilla	*Aralia nudicaulis*
American spikenard	American spikenard Indian root spignet	*Aralia racemosa*
angelica	angelica	*Angelica archangelica*
apple mint pineapple mint (when variegated) woolly mint monk's herb	pineapple mint (when variegated)	*Mentha rotundifolia*
arnica mountain tobacco	arnica	*Arnica montana*
artemisia	artemisia	*Artemisia* species
balsam	(known as Himalayan touch- me-not, but does not occur in the USA)	*Impatiens glandulifera* (syn. *I. roylei*)
basil sweet basil	sweet basil	*Ocymum basilicum*
bay sweet bay	sweet bay	*Laurus nobilis*
belladonna deadly nightshade banewort death's herb dwale deadly dwale sleeping nightshade	belladonna	*Atropa belladonna*
bergamot monarda bee balm balm	Oswego tea bee balm Indian plume fragrant balm mountain mint	*Monarda didyma*

ENGLISH	AMERICAN	BOTANICAL NAME
betony wood betony bishopswort wild hop	betony woundwort	*Stachys officinalis*
bistort snakeroot Easter ledges	bistort snakeweed	*Polygonum bistorta*
black horehound	black horehound	*Ballota nigra*
black peppermint	black peppermint	*Mentha × piperita vulgaris*
blackroot	Culver's root	*Leptandra virginica*
bloodroot	bloodroot red puccoon	*Sanguinaria canadensis*
borage bee-bread coll tankard herb of gladness	borage	*Borago officinalis*
Bowles's mint	Bowles's mint	*Mentha × villosa*
bryony cowhind cow's lick	bryony	*Brionica dioica*
burdock, great	cockle-bur beggar's buttons cuckoo button clot-bur	*Arctium lappa*
burnet	burnet	*Sanguisorba officinalis*
calamintha		*Calamintha* species
candytuft	candytuft	*Iberis amara*
caper spurge mole plant	caper spurge	*Euphorbia lathyris*
caraway	caraway	*Carum carvi*
carnation	carnation	*Dianthus caryophyllus*
catmint catnip	catnip	*Nepeta cataria*
celandine, greater swallow-wort killwart wartflower	celandine, greater	*Chelidonium majus*
celandine, lesser pilewort		*Ranunculus ficaria*
chamomile	chamomile bowman	*Anthemis nobilis*
cherry wild cherry gean	cherry	*Prunus* species
chervil	chervil	*Anthriscus cerefolium*
chicory bunk coffee weed French endive	chicory	*Cichorium intybus*
chives	chives	*Allium schoenoprasum*
cinquefoil		*Potentilla reptans*
clary		*Salvia horminum*
clary sage Christ's eye clear eye	clary sage	*Salvia sclarea*

ENGLISH	AMERICAN	BOTANICAL NAME
clematis	clematis	*Clematis vitalba*
coltsfoot hoofs tushy lucky gowan dummy weed coughwort	coltsfoot	*Tussilago farfara*
comfrey boneset knitbone consound	common comfrey knitbone blackwort	*Symphytum officinale*
coriander Chinese parsley	coriander cilandtro	*Coriandrum sativum*
corn mint	corn mint	*Mentha arvensis*
corn salad lamb's lettuce	corn salad	*Valerianella locusta*
cow parsley Cicely wild chervil		*Anthriscus sylvestris*
cowslip Our Lady's bunch of keys St Peter's keys palsywort	cowslip	*Primula veris*
cumin cummin	cumin	*Cuminum cyminum*
curry plant	curry plant	*Helichrysum angustifolium*
dandelion blowball peasant's clock cankerwort crow parsnip Irish daisy doon-head-clock fortune teller one o' clocks swine's snout	common dandelion blowball lion's tooth peasant's clock	*Taraxacum officinale*
Daphne mezereon	Daphne	*Daphne mezereum*
dill	dill	*Anethum graveolens*
dyer's rocket weld	dyer's rocket yellow weed weld	*Reseda luteole*
eau de cologne mint bergamot mint pineapple mint lemon mint	orange mint bergamot mint	*Mentha × piperita citrata*
elder elderberry eldern ellan elnorne	(known as European elder but does not occur in the USA)	*Sambucus nigra*
elecampane scabwort horse heal inula	elecampane horseheal yellow starwort	*Inula helenium*
evening primrose moonflower primrose tree moths	evening primrose night willow herb	*Oenothera biennis*
fennel	fennel	*Foeniculum vulgare*
fenugreek	fenugreek	*Trigonella foenum-graecum*

ENGLISH	AMERICAN	BOTANICAL NAME
feverfew	feverfew	*Chrysanthemum parthenium*
Florentine iris	Florentine iris	*Iris florentina*
foxglove fox fingers lady's thimble pop glove witches' bells bluidy man's fingers foxes gleow	foxglove thimble flower	*Digitalis purpurea*
fraxinella burning bush	false dittany fraxinella	*Dictamnus albus*
(French sorrel) (Buckler sorrel)	garden sorrel	*Rumex scutatus*
fritillary snake's head fritillary chequered daffodil chequered lily guinea-hen flower	fritillaria	*Fritillaria meleagris*
garlic	garlic	*Allium sativum*
gentian yellow gentian bitterwort baldmoney bitters	yellow gentian	*Gentiana lutea*
geranium		*Geranium* species
goat's rue	goat's rue	*Galega officinalis*
good King Henry Lincolnshire spinach Lincolnshire asparagus	good King Henry	*Chenopodium bonus-henricus*
ground ivy alehoof hayhoof tun hoof gill ale	ground ivy alehoof Gill-over-the-ground field balm creeping Charlie	*Glechoma hederacea*
hellebore Christmas rose	Christmas rose	*Helleborus niger*
hemlock herba benedicta herb bennet St Bennet's herb bad man's oatmeal bunk heck-how	poison hemlock	*Conium maculatum*
henbane loaves of bread chenile henbell stinking Roger belene bruisewort	henbane	*Hyoscyamus niger*
holy thistle milk thistle St Benedict's thistle		*Silybum marianum*
hop	European hop	*Humulus lupulus*
horse mint	horse mint	*Mentha longifolia*
horse radish	horse radish	*Armoracia rusticana*
hound's tongue gipsy flower rose noble dog's tongue	hound's tongue gipsy flower	*Cynoglossum officinale*

ENGLISH	AMERICAN	BOTANICAL NAME
houseleek hen-and-chickens huslock	houseleek hen-and-chickens	*Sempervivum tectorum*
hyssop	hyssop	*Hyssopus officinalis*
indigo	indigo	*Indigofera tinctoria*
iris, yellow flag flagons Jacob's sword	yellow flag	*Iris pseudacorus*
Jacob's Ladder Greek valerian	Jacob's Ladder	*Polemonium caeruleum*
Japanese mint	Japanese mint	*Mentha arvensis piperascens*
jasmine	jasmine	*Jasminum officinale*
jewel weed	spotted touch-me-not snapweed silver cap	*Impatiens capensis*
Jo Pye weed hemp agrimony	Jo Pye weed purple boneset trumpet weed purple throughout gravel weed kidney root	*Eupatorium cannabinum* *E. purpureum*
juniper	juniper hack matack horse savin	*Juniperus communis*
lady's mantle	lady's mantle	*Alchemilla vulgaris*
lavender	lavender	*Lavandula* species
lavender cotton cotton lavender	lavender cotton gray santolina	*Santolina chamaecyparissus*
lemon balm balm	lemon balm	*Melissa officinalis*
lemon verbena	lemon verbena	*Lippia citriodora*
licorice liquorice	licorice	*Glycyrrhiza glabra*
lily-of-the-valley	lily-of-the-valley	*Convallaria majalis*
lime lime tree	lime lime tree	*Tilia* species
lovage	lovage	*Levisticum officinale*
lungwort Jerusalem cowslip soldiers and sailors Adam and Eve Mary's milk drops spotted dog	lungwort	*Pulmonaria officinalis*
madder dyer's madder	madder	*Rubia tinctorum*
mallow	mallow	*Malva sylvestris*
marigold pot marigold Mary buds gold of ruddes	pot marigold	*Calendula officinalis*
marjoram	sweet marjoram	*Origanum* species
marshmallow	English mallow	*Althaea officinalis*
meadowsweet	meadowsweet queen of the meadow my lady's Bett	*Filipendula ulmaria*

ENGLISH	AMERICAN	BOTANICAL NAME
melilot	melilot	*Melilotus officinalis*
mignonette	common mignonette	*Reseda odorata*
milkwort	purple milkwort	*Polygala* species
monkshood aconite helmet flower old wife's hood	aconite	*Aconitum napellus*
motherwort	mugwort	*Artemisia vulgaria*
mullein Jacob's staff Jupiter's staff Peter's staff shepherd's staff candlewick plant blanket weed beggar's blanket felwort fluffweed old man's flannel	great mullein velvet plant flannel plant mullein dock common mullein Aaron's rod	*Verbascum thapsus*
musk mallow	musk mallow	*Malva moschata*
myrtle	myrtle	*Myrtus communis*
nasturtium	nasturtium	*Tropaeolum majus*
nettle stinging nettle	stinging nettle	*Urtica dioica*
nipplewort	nipplewort	*Lapsana communis*
onion	onion	*Allium cepa*
opium poppy	opium poppy	*Papaver somniferum*
parsley	parsley	*Petroselinum crispum*
pasque flower		*Pulsatilla vulgaris*
pelargonium	pelargonium	*Pelargonium* species
pellitory of the wall wallwort parietary Billie beatie lichwort		*Parietaria diffusa* (syn. *P. officinalis*)
pennyroyal	English pennyroyal	*Mentha pulegium*
peppermint	peppermint	*Mentha × piperita*
periwinkle sorcerer's violet	common periwinkle running myrtle	*Vinca* species
poppy cock rose redweed headache corn poppy	poppy corn poppy	*Papaver rhoeas*
purslane	purslane	*Portulaca oleracea*
pyrethrum	pyrethrum	*Pyrethrum coccineum*
queen of the prairie	queen of the prairie	*Filipendula rubra*
ramsons hog's garlic stink plant	(does not occur in the USA)	*Allium ursinum*
rhubarb	rhubarb	*Rheum officinale*
rose apothecary's rose rose of Provins	French rose rose of Provins gallica apothecary's rose	*Rosa gallica officinalis*

ENGLISH	AMERICAN	BOTANICAL NAME
rosemary	rosemary	*Rosmarinus officinalis*
rue	rue	*Ruta graveolens*
saffron	saffron	*Crocus sativus*
sage	sage garden sage	*Salvia officinalis*
St John's wort	St John's wort	*Hypericum perforatum*
samphire crestmarine	samphire	*Crithmum maritimum*
savory	savory	*Satureia* species
sea holly eryngo eryngium	eryngo sea holly	*Eryngium maritimum*
self heal all-heal hook heal brunella herb carpenter	all-heal self heal heart of the earth brunella seal heal	*Prunella vulgaris*
soapwort bouncing Bet fuller's herb crow soap latherwort bruisewort	soapwort bouncing Bet fuller's herb wild sweet William hedge pink old man's pink	*Saponaria officinalis*
Solomon's seal	Solomon's seal	*Polygonatum multiflorum*
sorrel French sorrel cuckoo meat	French sorrel	*Rumex acetosa*
southernwood lad's love old man maiden's ruin	southernwood lad's love	*Artemisia abrotanum*
spearmint mint garden mint spiremint green lamb mint Our Lady's mint	spear mint	*Mentha spicata*
spurge laurel wood laurel dwarf bay	spurge laurel	*Daphne laureola*
sunflower	sunflower	*Helianthus annuus*
sweet Cicely sweet fern British myrrh	sweet Cicely British myrrh	*Myrrhus odorata*
tansy	tansy	*Tanacetum vulgare*
tarragon, French estragon dragon's herb dragon's mugwort	French tarragon little tarragon	*Artemisia dracunculus*
tarragon, Russian	Russian tarragon	*Artemisia dracunculoides*
thistle	thistle	*Carduus benedictus*
thorn apple stramonium Jimson weed devil's apple devil's trumpet	thorn apple Jimson weed Jamestown weed devil's apple stramonium	*Datura stramonium*
thyme, common black thyme garden thyme	French thyme English thyme	*Thymus vulgaris*

ENGLISH	AMERICAN	BOTANICAL NAME
thyme, English wild thyme mother's thyme	creeping thyme mother of thyme	*Thymus serpyllum*
thyme, lemon German thyme winter thyme	thyme lemon thyme golden-edged thyme	*Thymus × citriodorus*
tobacco	tobacco	*Nicotiana tabacum*
valerian phu phew phew plant	garden heliotrope valerian	*Valeriana officinalis*
veratrum American white hellebore false hellebore green hellebore	American white hellebore itch weed green hellebore Indian poke	*Veratrum viride*
vervain herb of the cross holy vervain pigeon's meat	European vervain simpler's joy herb of the cross pigeon grass berbine	*Verbena officinalis*
violet sweet violet apple leaf bairn wort	English violet sweet violet March violet	*Viola odorata*
wall germander wood germander wood sage	germander	*Teucrium chamaedrys*
watercress well cress water cress broffin cress water crashes teng-tongue	watercress	*Nasturtium officinale*
water mint mint	water mint fish mint apple mint	*Mentha aquatica*
Welsh onion	Welsh onion	*Allium fistulosum*
white horehound	common horehound	*Marrubium vulgare*
white peppermint		*Mentha × piperita officinalis*
wild strawberry	wild strawberry	*Fragaria vesca*
willow herb rosebay fireweed	great willow herb spiked willow herb fireweed	*Chamaenerion angustifolium*
wintergreen partridge berry Canada tea tea berry	wintergreen mountain tea ground tea tea berry spice berry checker-berry	*Gaultheria procumbens*
witch hazel	witch hazel	*Hamamelis virginiana*
woodruff sweet woodruff	sweet woodruff	*Asperula odorata*
wormwood absinth waremouth mugwort	common wormwood	*Artemisia absinthium*
yarrow sneezewort nosebleed devil's nettle old man's pepper	sneezewort yarrow nosebleed milfoil	*Achillea millefolium*